27

Authentic Assessment
PRIMER

PETER LANG
New York • Washington, D.C./Baltimore • Bern
Frankfurt am Main • Berlin • Brussels • Vienna • Oxford

Valerie J. Janesick

Authentic Assessment
PRIMER

PETER LANG
New York • Washington, D.C./Baltimore • Bern
Frankfurt am Main • Berlin • Brussels • Vienna • Oxford

Library of Congress Cataloging-in-Publication Data

Janesick, Valerie J.
Authentic assessment primer / Valerie J. Janesick.
p. cm.
Includes bibliographical references.
1. Educational evaluation. 2. Educational surveys.
3. Educational tests and measurements—Evaluation. I. Title.
LB2822.75.J36   371.26—dc22   2005032909
ISBN 0-8204-7648-X

Bibliographic information published by **Die Deutsche Bibliothek**.
Die Deutsche Bibliothek lists this publication in the "Deutsche
Nationalbibliografie"; detailed bibliographic data is available
on the Internet at http://dnb.ddb.de/.

371.26 JANESIC 2006

Janesick, Valerie J.

Authentic assessment primer

Cover design by Lisa Barfield

The paper in this book meets the guidelines for permanence and durability
of the Committee on Production Guidelines for Book Longevity
of the Council of Library Resources.

© 2006 Peter Lang Publishing, Inc., New York
29 Broadway, New York, NY 10006
www.peterlang.com

Printed in the United States of America

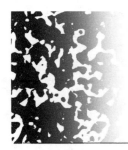

Table of Contents

Introduction and Overview

The dogmas of the quiet past are inadequate to the stormy present. The occasion is piled high with difficulty, and we must rise with the occasion. As our case is new, so we must think anew and act anew.

Abraham Lincoln
Second Annual Message to Congress
December 1, 1862

High-stakes testing
standardized tests whose results are used as the basis of important decisions, such as decreasing a school's funding or retaining a student in a grade level

Authentic assessment
requires authentic tasks that show students' abilities. Students receive feedback and redirection to allow for growth; students have a part in the process and the outcome

I first became interested in authentic assessment when in the mid-1990s I was visiting schools in a major urban school system and heard teachers complain of the trauma, upset, and just plain silliness of **high-stakes testing**. I suppose you might say that it was due to high-stakes testing that I decided to write about **authentic assessment** (Janesick 2001). Since then I have been increasingly concerned about the continuing emphasis on high-stakes testing despite what we know of its harm and biases. In addition, the systemic attack on public education which began in the 1980s with the Reagan administration has not abated. In fact, it has intensified as a corporate

model of profiteering has replaced an emphasis on learning, child development studies, and research which clearly shows how disadvantaged populations in particular have suffered due to high-stakes standardized tests. Of course, if we assume that schools reflect society, one only has to look around at the politics of the day. It is no wonder that schools are being cast as miniature corporations with a one-size-fits-all model of education and testing. When I wrote *The Assessment Debate* (2001), I could never imagine that I would be living and working in Florida—a highly controversial high-stakes testing state—sitting down to write another book on this topic. I am rethinking many of my earlier writings and reshaping them here. I like to think of this primer as a journey. It is being written for those who want to learn about the importance and value of authentic assessment and is presented as a real alternative to high-stakes testing.

Let us begin with a vignette recently reported in the *St. Petersburg Times* of Florida on February 10, 2005, by Lane DeGregory. I have summarized the article as it is a befitting beginning to this journey. The title reads "For sick kids, FCAT's just another exam." Here we learn about George Purvis, Jr.,who was injured in a biking accident. George had to drag himself to take the 10th grade Florida Comprehensive Assessment Test, "FCAT," even though he was unable to hold a No. 2 pencil required for the test. Luckily, he was a creative fellow: He used wrapped tape around the pencil until he could grasp it enough to fill in the 54 bubbles on the test paper. Of course, he had to ignore the spasms in his back and literally scratch out an essay with his weakened left hand. But did you know that each year in Florida, many sick and injured kids take the FCAT? Kids on dialysis, in casts, with transplants, with new bone marrow transplants, with broken necks, with Chemo drips, and with crippling burns.

George has since made significant strides in his rehabilitation. He stumbles in the shower, and his dad ties his shoes, but he no longer needs a diaper or a wheel chair. Though the FCAT exam totally

exhausted him, George knew that the next battery of tests awaited him in two weeks. Keep this case in mind as we wind through this journey on authentic assessment.

Overview

As a result of their dissatisfaction with typical standardized tests, high-stakes testing, and a misplaced emphasis on rote repetition suggestive of a nostalgia for the "olden days," many professionals, researchers, and educators have begun to search for a better way to assess student work. Starting in the 1980s, the authentic assessment movement has evolved and is alive and well today. Educators and researchers relentlessly have concentrated on authentic assessment to determine whether students can explain, apply, and critique their own responses and justify the answers they provide. In addition, authentic assessment is dynamic and looks at what students should be able *to do,* how they continually learn, and how they progress through their studies. It is most like the process in the arts with critique, feedback, redirection, and reconstruction. Authentic assessment stands in contrast to typical tests. Typical tests are known by the following traits:

1 Usually require one and only one correct response;
2 Usually are disconnected from the individual student's environment;
3 Usually are constructed by a bureaucrat removed from the student's environment;
4 The test maker may in fact *not be knowledgeable* about the field in which questions are being constructed;
5 Usually are simplified for ease in scoring;
6 Provide a one-shot, one-time score.

Many educators were dissatisfied with this approach to testing and evaluating students. Thus a new way of defining and viewing assessment has been taking shape. This new approach is called authentic assessment.

What Is Authentic Assessment?

There are numerous books and articles on authentic assessment. Many writers have devoted their lives to examining assessment, offering strong criticism against standardized tests, and giving reasonable alternatives to uniform standardized tests. Writers such as Grant Wiggins (1993, 1999), Alfie Kohn (2000, 2004), Ray Horn and Joe Kincheloe, (2001), Mark Goldberg (2005), and Susan Ohanian (1999) have published numerous books and articles on the topic (listed in the references to this book). Wiggins (1998) suggests the following standards for authentic assessment. An assessment task is authentic when:

1   It is realistic. The assessment task should follow closely the ways in which a person's abilities are "tested" in the real world. For example, as a former dancer, we practiced dance exercises such as plies, jetes, turns, and so on in ballet class. These are merely exercises, though. The realistic assessment task would be found in the actual performance of the ballet. In the *Nutcracker Suite Ballet,* as a cast member, I was forced to show what I could do. This is a realistic test, an authentic assessment measure.

2   It requires judgment and innovation. Here the student must use knowledge and skills to solve problems.

3   It asks the student to *do* the subject. Back to the ballet dancer, the dancer must put all the steps together and perform a role in an actual ballet.

4   It replicates or simulates actual "tests" in the workplace, personal life, and civic life. Because each student is at a unique stage of growth and development at any given time, why authentic assessment is more sensible than contrived standardized tests is easily appreciated. For one thing, one size does not fit all students. Common sense surely indicates this.

5   It assesses the student's ability and skills to effectively and efficiently use a repertoire of many skills to complete a problem or task. In

terms of accessing more than verbal or mathematical skills, authentic assessment relies on all the many intelligences a person can develop. Later in this chapter, I will take up the work of Howard Gardner (1993, 1999) on the topic of **multiple intelligences**.

Multiple intelligences

a theory formulated by Howard Gardner, according to which the concept of intelligence includes musical, bodily-kiesthetic, locigal-mathematical, spatial, interpersonal, intrapersonal, and linguistic forms of intelligence

---

6 It allows many opportunities to practice, rehearse, consult, get feedback, and refine actual performances and productions. Thus we have performance, feedback, performance revision, feedback, performance, and so on. In other words, students must learn something and get better at doing the task at hand. In many ways this is like the artist who has constant critique for improvement. To use dance as an example once again, after each performance, the director of a performance piece typically reads "critique notes" at the end of every performance. Thus built into the concept of feedback is the assumption that the student will work to improve the next performance test.

The reason authentic assessment is important is obvious. Every teacher is forced to assess the achievement and progress of students. Because teachers deal with assessment issues constantly, educators

CHARACTERISTICS OF TYPICAL TESTS AND AUTHENTIC TASKS

Typical Test	Authentic Task
Requires correct answer	Requires quality performance or product
Is disconnected from the student's environment	Is connected to the student's world
Is simplified	Is complex and multilayered
Is one-shot	Is continuing with multiple tasks
Provides one score	Provides complex feedback continually recurring; as the student self-adjusts, performance is improved.
Looks for one level of thinking	Looks for higher-order skills with a demonstration of knowledge.

in every arena want to find a realistic, workable, and authentic system of assessment. Similarly, the reader can appreciate the difference between typical tests and authentic assessment as listed on page 5.

Thus, an authentic assessment task is designed to provide a richer, stronger, and more complex approach to understanding student progress. The actual performance or production usually tells us about what the student has been learning. It also provides a way for students and teachers to keep track of the student's progress. When authentic assessment is used, the student must provide evidence of some growth and improvement. It is an approach to assessment whose time has come. It stands in contrast to typical tests. In typical testing, one cannot always be sure that growth has taken place. If a student crams for a test and memorizes facts to be recalled once on a one-shot test, how can we know exactly what was learned? Because the typical test is usually testing some facts devoid of the student's actual experience or social context, how can we assume the student learned?

Issues Regarding the Use of Assessment

The field of assessment today is rich with writing and research in the following areas:

1   The nature of the use of assessment;
2   The need for displaying how students think, learn, pose, and solve problems;
3   The need to focus on student achievements within reason and common sense;
4   The correct balance, case by case, school by school, between performance-based authentic assessment and the use of standardized testing; and
5   Delineating the concerns and problems with standardized tests. These concerns include:
    a   Schools and districts may not be reporting data accurately. The literature is filled with examples on the way some test reporters get around accurate reporting. Consequently, the data reported are inaccurate and can be used deceptively.

b Some teachers are pressured into only teaching to the test. Consequently, the regular curriculum is abandoned for drilling for the test.

c The pressure to report test scores publicly in newspapers, for example, can divide communities and individuals. Most often poor, underfunded schools have lower test scores on standardized tests.

d Test bias against various ethnic groups, females, limited English proficiency students, low-income students, and special needs students exists.

e Testing is extremely costly. Considerable school district resources go into the high cost of standardized testing. This takes money from other worthy budget categories like teacher development or classroom materials. The testing industry has become a multibillion dollar industry which profits test makers. Usually, the test maker is in another state and, in fact, scoring of the standardized high-stakes test is done in yet another state removed from the local context. Other problems with the profiteering aspects of high-stakes testing may involve, as in Florida, conflicts of interest for public figures. In Florida, the high-stakes standardized test is called the FCAT, and at one time, Neil Bush, the brother of the current governor of Florida and the brother of President George W. Bush, through his software company IGNITE, exploited his other brother's **No Child Left Behind Act (NCLB)** education strategy by owning all aspects of the FCAT. Due to numerous threats of impropriety and lawsuits, it appears that the FCAT is now owned by McGraw Hill. Still the Neil Bush operation, under the Web site www.ignite-learning.com is still up and running. One wonders how and why McGraw Hill came to this arrangement.

No Child Left Behind Act (NCLB)

NCLB requires adequate yearly progress (AYP) on state tests in major subjects every year. The law is highly controversial because it is not meeting its stated purpose by just about any measure

f The illusion that something is getting better in a school based on a test score is extremely misleading.

g Last but not least, one-size testing does not fit all.

Thus, discussions continue on these critical points and are the heart and soul of the value and usefulness of authentic assessment. First, though, we need to understand the history of the assessment movement.

The History of Assessment

Public schools in the United States have always been scrutinized. In many of his writings John Dewey (1859–1952) underscored the issues involved in the public aspect of education, the complexity of learning processes. Actually, Dewey was a philosopher of education who early on recognized the importance of what we now call "authentic assessment." Indeed, his ideas are the basis for today's authentic assessment.

Let me back up, then, and explain the profound influence in education of the philosopher and activist, John Dewey. He certainly provided the foundations for authentic assessment in many ways. Dewey is widely recognized as the most powerful influence in educational philosophy and practice. His pragmatism, that branch of philosophy which seeks to balance theory and practice, with an eye to social change, caused schooling to change and curriculum specialists to rejoice. Dewey began the Laboratory School at the University of Chicago between 1896–1904. He wanted to see theory in action and the importance of experience in education. In fact, he claimed that we cannot know something without directly experiencing it. Surely this is one major idea that frames authentic assessment. For example, you learn about becoming a ballet dancer by actually taking classes in ballet, by learning anatomy for the dancer, by learning how to critique and analyze ballets, and then actually performing in a ballet before an audience and the artistic director. You would not only read a book about ballet to learn ballet. To use another example, children at early ages learn mathematical principles by using handheld

objects or manipulatives, or various objects to work with. All of us who love literature love it because vicariously we experience the world of the writer. While Dewey historically falls in the time period of the Traditionalists and Reconceptualists, he foreshadows and influences the postmodern writers as well. Thus, in terms of assessment, Dewey has provided current researchers and writers with a strong foundation.

Dewey's groundbreaking work in the following texts helped to shape some of our schools then and now, here and around the world. Of his voluminous writings, these texts in particular relate to authentic assessment:

1   *My Pedagogic Creed* (1897)
2   *The School and Society* (1899)
3   *The Child and the Curriculum* (1902)
4   *How We Think* (1910)
5   *Art as Experience* (1934)
6   *Experience and Education* (1938)

In addition to these primary resources, many texts have been written about Dewey's work. Still to this day, educators are actively attempting to put into practice Dewey's ideas, principles, and practices. Dewey was the first to argue for what would later be a major shift from control of subject matter by the teacher, *to control of learning by the student*. This idea alone could be considered a seed for what currently is called authentic assessment. In addition, he preferred a balanced give-and-take posture between student and teacher. This was preferable to a technocratic, spoon-fed curriculum. Throughout Dewey's life and beyond, his writings influenced thinkers in philosophy, history, education, and the arts. In education, his most enduring legacy in terms of assessment includes his focus on:

1   Experience as a key element in the educative process;
2   Child-centered activities for learning in the early years;
3   Democracy and education;

4 The significance of art as experience and a key component of education;

5 Awareness of the importance of the public school as a key element of educating the citizenry for a healthy democracy;

6 Pragmatism or the balance between theory and practice;

7 Progressivism, or the movement to ensure experience-based education, a move away from technocratic approaches to curriculum, toward dealing with the whole child. Not only that, progressivism also had a goal of social improvement and change. For the first time, educators were looking to the school and society as never before. Thus the idea of social justice emerges early in the history of education, although this fact is regularly overlooked.

8 The school must be a community. (It was this idea that the postmodernists took up and amplified.). Dewey focused on the importance of the context in which a student learns something. The school provided a sense of connectedness and community at the time he was writing about these ideas.

9 Ethical treatment of students and teachers. Dewey firmly believed that trickery should not be used in education. Later in this text, I will speak to the attempt to trick students into "wrong" answers on standardized tests.

Each of these categories is a precursor of authentic assessment. Dewey had many ideas congruent with other great thinkers worldwide such as Jean Piaget (1898–1980), the Swiss psychologist, and Maria Montessori (1870–1952), the Italian medical doctor and educator. Furthermore the Austrian philosopher Rudolf Steiner (1861–1925) held these beliefs. Dewey's thought, writing and Laboratory School most certainly affected many educators then and now. In addition, Dewey's text *Democracy and Education* (1916/1966) was recently named by an extremist group of noneducators led by William Bennett, as the fifth most dangerous book ever writ-

ten. It is presumed that this group was worried about the fact that literacy is critical to a democracy.

How the Social Context Changed

However, since the 1950s a number of writers have been concerned with learning and the measurement of what is learned. As our nation focused on business, private enterprise, and making profits, that same kind of thinking was beginning to be used to evaluate schools. Likewise, calls for reforms in education began in the 1980s when students were described as illiterate. Berliner and Biddle (1995), two well-known educators and researchers, explain how the 1980s were filled with reports attacking teachers and schools. These attacks were baseless and relied on hearsay rather than actual evidence. They were part of a well organized propaganda campaign against public schools in an effort to advance an agenda of privatization of schools to favor a corporate money-making model often at the expense of children. Berliner and Biddle uncovered several myths which sparked the continuation of the assessment movement. The myths they exposed include:

1   Student achievement in American primary schools has recently declined. In fact, the authors found no evidence for this claim.
2   The performance of American college students has recently fallen. Again, the authors found no evidence to support this claim.
3   The intellectual, abstract thinking, and problem-solving skills of American youths have declined. Once again, the writers have found no evidence to support this claim and in fact have found evidence that shows American students' abilities are not in decline.

What is critical to remember here is that the *public perception* of our schools is affected by newspaper and popular media reports whether or not there is evidence to support these negative reports. Educators consequently have gone on the offensive and taken

up the reform agenda. They want to seriously:

1 Make schools better for students;
2 Provide meaningful and appropriate instruction for each grade level;
3 Design authentic assessment tasks which truly show what students can do and what they learn from their studies;
4 Respond to critics of public schools with solid, demonstrable results;
5 Organize in local communities to fight the one-shot, commercial, high-stakes tests usually disconnected from the curriculum.

We are at an exciting and hopeful time in this era of educational reform. Many researchers are making great strides in discovering how the mind operates and how children learn. To take just one example, the renowned Harvard physician and researcher Howard Gardner has devoted his lifetime to discovering, describing, and explaining how the mind works and how we learn. By doing this, he illuminates the value of authentic assessment. Gardner has done more than anyone in this area of multiple intelligences and how to assess them. His documentation of multiple intelligences illuminates our understanding of how the mind works amd argues that the mind and the learning process are complex. Up to now, we have been relying on tests that are narrow, limited, and one-shot ordeals to evaluate learning. Furthermore, he argues that we must try to understand the full range of human intelligence to evaluate how we learn in order to survive. According to him, intelligence is more than the ability to give correct answers on a test. He claims intelligence entails the ability to solve problems or fashion products that are important in a particular cultural setting. In fact, he describes eight intelligences:

1 Musical intelligence;
2 Bodily kinesthetic intelligence;
3 Logical-mathematical intelligence;
4 Linguistic intelligence;
5 Spatial intelligence;

6   Interpersonal intelligence;

7   Intrapersonal intelligence;

8   Naturalist intelligence.

If we look at each of these, it is clear that what we have been doing for years in testing and assessment is inadequate. Thus, the authentic assessment movement naturally evolved and continues to gain strength and momentum. In addition, a tremendously powerful grassroots movement against high-stakes testing is growing among professional organizations, parents, educators, private citizens, and students themselves. Later in this text I will describe some of the key resources in terms of Internet Web sites which document this grassroots movement against high-stakes testing. In fact, the states of California, Massachusetts, Ohio, Iowa, Arizona, Florida, Georgia, Maryland, Michigan, North Carolina, New York, Ohio, Texas, Virginia, and Washington have documented their strategies for all to see by constructing Web sites with links to action steps, letters to Congress, and parent education programs to inform the public about the harmful effects of the current money-making, high-stakes testing industry. Can we ever forget the boycott in Minnesota on testing after all fourth graders failed the math test? How about the response by the high-stakes test makers, whose only answer to this improbable occurrence amounted to "oops we made a mistake in scoring." Then there is the example of the standardized Massachusetts teacher test where virtually all the teachers failed? Similarly, in Michigan educators had to lower the bar on their standardized tests as they were set too high to accommodate the federal score. Thus Michigan officials basically dumbed down the standardized test in high school English proficiency to avoid losing federal money and avoid looking like a "failure." Again, the test makers could only come up with, in effect, an "oops we made a mistake" explanation. It is no surprise that at this moment in time, authentic assessment is gaining prominence given all these shenanigans. With the use of authentic tasks, we can do justice to the com-

Performance-based assessment

this term is often used interchangeably with authentic assessment. It is assessment based on performance tasks designed to show what a student can do, such as making a movie, performing a dance, writing an essay, constructing art work, preparing demonstrations, sharing journal writing, or conducting an interview

plexity of learning. Authentic assessment provides educators with a space to truly address what students know and how student knowledge can be applied in an actual **performance-based assessment.** That knowledge can more easily document what was learned, as well as monitor the student's progress.

Put simply, authentic assessment goes beyond what a student knows to what a student *can do.* Let's examine this more closely and contrast this to typical texts. Most educators agree that the reform movement of the 1980s and 1990s began the serious questioning of testing, as we thought we knew it. The basic issue that was on the minds of reformers was whether traditionally administered tests actually test the information children learn in school. Needless to say, the answer in many cases was a resounding "no." Consequently, authentic assessment offered teachers a valuable tool. This tool was used to evaluate learning in the settings closely related to the real world. Furthermore, students had to give reasons for their answers. They had to provide evidence they fully understood the concepts. It allowed for active learning on the students' part. Multiple indicators were used to show that students actually understood the content under study. Students had to use their judgment and powers of reason. At the same time, they had to explain and evaluate their work and responses to the problems. They had to demonstrate what they learned.

Throughout the 1990s, many writers argued that typical tests offered very poor content coverage and emphasized a narrow range of cognitive skills. In addition, many of the tests given to children were removed from the child's actual experience. It is not surprising, then, that authentic assessment became a powerful beacon of light. Wiggins (1993a) and others saw the value of how performance-based authentic assessment had been traditionally used in the arts, music, and many vocational education classes. In these disciplines, students almost always use authentic assessment procedures. The music student, for example, must ultimately *play* the concerto on the piano or actually *compose* a musical piece.

The student of drawing must deliver real drawings for review. The student studying mechanics must perform a mechanical task for evaluation. Thus, in order to be authentic, assessments must have meaning in themselves. Whatever learning they measure, authentic assessments *must be meaningful to the student.* On the other hand, conventional test designers do the opposite of authentic assessment. One researcher, Lauren Resnick (1990), pointed out that the two key assumptions of conventional test design are both false and problematic:

1   The notion that we can decompose elements of knowledge, and
2   The notion that we can decontextualize knowledge sends a non-educative message.

We simply cannot continue to make false assumptions about learning given what we know through research and practice. These two assumptions only punctuate Wiggins's and other writers' entreaty that we are not preparing our students for the messy real world. As Wiggins retells a constant teacher complaint, "The trouble with kids today is that they don't know what to do when they don't know what to do." As we think about this, let us turn to a brief history of the evolution of the assessment movement.

The Theoretical Basis for Assessment

The current assessment movement can easily trace its origins to the intellectual movement known as postmodernism. It was at the time of World War I that standardized testing was used to sort army recruits. It was not long before bureaucrats sought to use the techniques of the army designed for adults as a catch-all for the efficiency movement. Bureaucrats thought that if testing worked for the army, it can work for schools. Enter the era of the postmodernists. Many sociologists chart the beginning of postmodernism to World War II. They point to the atomic bombing of Hiroshima and Nagasaki as a critical turning point in history. It is as a result of the atomic bomb that key writers, artists, philosophers,

world leaders, educators, and citizens began to raise serious questions regarding Western ways of thinking and doing business.

Postmodernism

Postmodernism is a theoretical framework and a form of critique that questions the following assumptions:

1　The primacy and legitimacy of Western reason and its social political, economic, and educational effects without an understanding of how these values affect other nations;
2　Obligatory Western heroes who presuppose a privilege for these heroes, often resulting in some form of unethical behavior self-justified by this privilege, which in turn reinforces a double-standard that the West can critique others but cannot itself be a genuine target of criticism;
3　Stories of colonialism, expansionism, progress, and the success of science which neglect the working poor, minorities, and the erosion of the environment leading to, in many cases, a denial of class, race, and gender issues in schools and society;
4　Western ideologies that locate the non-Westerner as the "problem."

If we take a postmodern view of schooling, one of the main concerns of the educator is to attempt to uncover ways how dominant schooling practices serve to perpetuate the hopelessness of the oppressed. As a result, those who conduct assessment from a postmodern perspective demand a framework that:

1　Recognizes the power of race, class, and gender differences and how these shape educational outcomes;
2　Exposes the ways power works to structure inequality;
3　Promotes a narrative of hope, complexity, and multiple competing perceptions of social reality;
4　Conceptualizes ways which promote a more human and hopeful approach to school, work,

parenting, play, and so on;

5 Understands that all teachers are students and all students are teachers;

6 Realizes that no one single vision of the world is enough to change the world;

7 Demands that assessment of students be fair;

8 Allows children to be children and to progress through the stages of development without thinking of children as miniature adults.

Basically, the authentic assessment movement is a commonsense approach to evaluating students with an awareness of child development and how students learn. It confirms what a student *can do*. It is connected to each student's experience in education.

Postmodernism and Alternative Approaches to Schooling and Assessment

Another trend related to Postmodernism is that of alternative schooling approaches. Alternative approaches include all the private schools, charter schools, and home schooling. The brief descriptions of the major alternative approaches discussed in the following section include home schooling, the Waldorf schools, and the Montessori schools. (Parochial and religious-based schools are a topic for another author at another time.) However, these three approaches to alternative schooling are important to understand in today's context as most of them do not, in fact, participate at all in any high-stakes testing. Would it not be amazing for public schools to also opt out of high-stakes testing? I mention this here to stress that we might learn something from these alternative models.

Home Schooling as an Alternative

Home schooling has historical roots prior to the industrialization of the nineteenth century. At that time, most American families were centered on the daily home-based activities of an agrarian lifestyle. In addition to teaching their children how to grow crops and tend to livestock, parents sometimes

taught their youngsters how to read, write, and do arithmetic. In 1852, Massachusetts enacted the first compulsory school attendance law. At about that same time, the first child labor laws were also being passed as the United States shifted from being an agrarian society to that of being an industrialized nation. Public schools gained popularity, and by the end of the nineteenth century, American children were becoming accustomed to government-sponsored compulsory education.

The origins of the contemporary home schooling movement can be linked to the outcry for school reform beginning in the 1960s. At that time, educational reformers began challenging school methodology and criticizing academic outcomes such as test scores. Among those who called for reform were Paul Goodman, John Holt, Charles E. Silberman, and Ivan Illich—each of whom contributed to a now-classic series of critiques: *Compulsory Miseducation* (Goodman 1962), *How Children Fail* (Holt 1964), *Crisis in the Classroom: The Remaking of American Education* (Silberman 1970), and *Deschooling Society* (Illich 1971). Subsequently, Dr. Raymond and Dorothy Moore, authors of *Home Grown Kids: A Practical Handbook for Teaching Your Children at Home* (1981) began encouraging home schooling among members of the religious right. By the mid-1980s, increasing numbers of home schooling proponents were pressuring state legislators to rewrite compulsory school attendance statutes. As a result of these efforts, all 50 states, the District of Columbia, Puerto Rico, and other U.S. territories now have rules about home schooling. In fact, home schooling is a legal alternative in all 50 states, and in the U.S. Territories.

Today it is estimated that up to about 800,000 students are home schooled in the United States. What began as part of a religious movement for a small group has gained popularity among mainstream Americans. Indeed, just as home schooling laws vary from state to state, the reasons for educating children at home vary considerably among parents. Many claim that schooling their children at home offers a safer, more secure, more moral, and more disciplined environment of higher educational quality. Many involved in home schooling cite the importance of child development and the need for security, emotional closeness, and flexibility in schooling as some of the best reasons for home schooling. However, home schooling has developed to offer more than simply comfort, safety, and security. Currently, guidebooks, textbooks, and other teaching materials—much like those in public schools—are available for home schooling.

While home schooling may work for some, there is continuing criticism of the movement if only because it was originally adopted and pursued by the fundamentalist Christian right. They wanted to use home schooling as a tool to take their children out of the public schools due to concerns regarding violence, moral values, and other issues. As a result, the movement was severely criticized as many home schoolers were without texts, teachers, and so on, and were in fact tantamount to something like informal Bible study. Thus, reformers who saw the real value of home schooling began to work with educators, various state departments of education, and parents to revise how home schooling might take shape and helped redirect a small group of eccentric approaches toward a more formal, organized, and content-rich curriculum. All indicators in the literature indicate that home schooling is growing due to its allure and successes. In fact, many home schooling parents write about the performance-based tasks they use to prove what they can do.

The Montessori Model: Schooling and Curriculum

The noted educator, physician, and activist Maria Montessori (1870–1952) discovered that children who were orphans, disabled, and abandoned could be educated with a caring approach to education. The Montessori method includes direct hands-on experience, learning by doing, and education of the whole child. Montessori believed that children learn best when they are exploring like scientists performing experiments rather than passively accepting ideas. In the Montessori school environment,

children initiate learning and socialization voluntarily. Meanwhile, teachers permit the children to interact with their planned environment and with each other without expectations or scrutiny. The rationale of Montessori education is based on an integrated philosophy: children are respected as individuals and as being different from adults; children possess a special sensitivity and an unusual intellectual ability to absorb and learn from their environment; and the first six years are the most important years of a child's development. For these reasons, Montessori schools are geared for elementary school aged children.

Montessori educators design and direct the learning environment by preparing it in advance to be a positive and safe social atmosphere. They provide children with copious educational materials that emphasize concrete versus abstract learning. According to proponents, the children work for the joy of learning and discovery. There often is a three year age span of children in the classroom, with older children teaching the younger ones. This structure in itself often helps with development. Beyond maintaining certain rules for safety and mutual respect, teachers play a relatively unobtrusive role in the classroom. Teachers are facilitators. However, they control the environment by organizing what learning materials are available for the children, and they serve as a resource and role model in the classroom.

Today there are thousands of Montessori schools worldwide. In the United States, there are approximately 5,000 Montessori schools. While some opponents complain that Montessori schools are too rigid, others claim that Montessori schools are too permissive, letting children run around doing whatever they will. Indeed, the Montessori method is geared to providing experiences from which children will learn. Many of the classroom activities focus on the development of social skills, physical coordination, and performance-based assessments. However, the Montessori classroom takes a relatively holistic approach to the curriculum by permitting children to learn through their natural curiosity. Similar to

home schooling, the focus is on safety, caring, experimenting, and communication. A third alternative model of schooling with characteristics similar to home schooling is the Waldorf model.

Rudolf Steiner and the Waldorf Schools

The first of the Waldorf schools opened in 1919 in Stuttgart, Germany, for the children of factory workers. By 1928, the first Waldorf school opened in New York City, and still others followed in North America. (They are called Waldorf schools because the factory where the first school was located was the Waldorf-Astoria cigarette factory.) Today, there are around 700 schools in 40 countries worldwide. Rudolf Steiner ran the original school based on his understanding of the true purposes of schooling in the modern era. Steiner emphasized intuition, creativity, movement, dance, the arts, and thinking as requirements for children to grow and develop. Due to World War I, Steiner was taken with questions about creating a better society. He wondered about creating a free society with ethics and responsibility. True to this spirit, a Waldorf school balances academics, the arts, and character development with a sense of community responsibility. Because students stay with the same teacher for up to eight years, a true learning community is constantly developing. Steiner wrote numerous books and articles on child learning, development, and his method.

Steiner coined the term "anthroposophy" which he defined as a spiritual movement for educating the whole person. This educational philosophy ran counter to the norms of the day which followed a traditional approach to education. In addition, another term, "eurythmy," is a key term for the Waldorf schools. Eurythmy is defined as speaking and singing through movement and gestures for the purpose of getting children in touch with their own rhythm and the world around them. It was believed to be therapeutic as well. By including this in the curriculum, Steiner envisioned eurythmy as a way for children to acknowledge and name their own feel-

ings. Waldorf schools and their goals are about head, heart, and hands in order to develop individuals who are able to impart meaning to their lives. Moreover, the Waldorf schools use student-made texts, tests, and performance-based assessments to chart what a student can do. The Anthroposophic Press (*www.anthropress.org*) is a good resource on Waldorf schools and Steiner's creative approach to the curriculum as well as research on Waldorf Schools.

Thus, we have three examples of alternative approaches that comfortably use authentic assessment as a day-to-day reality. All three depart from the traditional norms of testing children. All three approaches offer a wider perspective in terms of educating the whole child, encouraging communication, and fostering a sense of community, meaning in one's life, and responsibility for actions. Ethics becomes part of the entire educational process. All three approaches offer educators something to think about in their own worlds. Each may serve to inspire curriculum and assessment professionals in their current settings to broaden their understanding of what is possible in terms of authentic assessment. In a way, postmodernism, enables us to examine our own practices to see alternatives that go beyond the present. Similarly, the hot-button issues involving educational reform will always have a component that has to do with evaluation, assessment of practice, and finding and making sense of that practice. Thus, postmodern trends include assessment and standards as key issues for school reform, the next logical step for attempting reform and change. To understand, then, authentic assessment more fully, we need to understand how it fits with the standards movement and reforms of the day.

School Reform, Standards, and Assessment

Looking back at the history of the standards movement, it is often linked to the educational reform movement sparked by the report "A Nation at Risk" (1983). Of course, we can easily claim that educational reform has been a pastime for over a cen-

tury, as many writers have done (e.g., Cuban 1990). However, individual educators, and professional organizations are now demanding standards as a remedy to almost every educational problem. Consider the points regarding school reform recently elucidated by Orlich (2000), an educator and leader challenging this reform movement.

While school reform might be defined as "anything you can get away with," the bulk of reforms in the United States seem to exhibit eight general characteristics:

1   The reforms are politically inspired and coerced by state governments. They are usually tied to federal funding;

2   The stress on higher student achievement is based on standards-based reports that are prepared by non-educators and persons not trained in child development;

3   Content standards tend to be collections of outcomes or student behaviors, assembled in a nonsystematic manner without clearly delineated hierarchies;

4   Cost-benefit analyses are not provided in the reports on state school reforms. (In fact, the excessive cost of high-stakes testing connected to the standards movement is highly suspicious.)

5   Control of education has shifted to national and state levels, away from localities;

6   The reform agendas, though fragmentary, are broad in scale and encompass most of the 50 states;

7   Politically inspired as the education reform movement has been, it must still be classified as being without theory; that is, its basic premises are grounded not in empirically sound studies but rather in political enthusiasms and intuitions.

8   Implied within these reforms and standards is the conclusion that, as a consequence of standards and high-stakes state testing and assessment programs, there should be a dramatic increase in student achievement.

The time has come to revisit the premise that massive funding, written standards, and a firm resolve to create "reform" will cause students to achieve at higher levels. For one, there are developmental limits to student achievement. Nevertheless, as some writers have argued, the notion of setting high standards for all students is hard to resist. After all, it is difficult to argue against high standards. However, if we go deeply into the complex issues related to standards, this truism obscures more than it reveals. Why are we so enticed by conversations on standards and authentic assessment today? A look at the following timeline may be helpful.

A Timeline for the Evolution of Assessment

1946–1960   Postmodernism takes root in all disciplines, especially art, dance, drama, language, literature, science, business, philosophy, law, and the humanities in general. Public education enjoys a period of relative calm. After Sputnik, politicians seek to emphasize science and mathematics in school programs. Teachers begin to organize more effectively, and unions play a stronger role. Teachers also make their own tests based on the content covered in classes.

1960s–1970s   The Civil Rights Movement, the Feminist Movement, the Gay Liberation Movement, and the Children's Rights Movement make their voices and agenda known. Educational reformers begin to question how schools work. In particular, the Vietnam conflict and the deep division in the country over it, as well as distrust of politicians due to Nixon's resignation, oddly enough, boost teachers' efforts to teach for learning and understanding. It is in this period that child development is seriously considered in the making of teacher-made tests. The literature in psychology by volume alone suggests a serious belief that the whole child should be educated. It suggests that schools should be more like communities with an ethic of care for individuals.

1970s   Howard Gardner begins a thirty-year period of

research on how the mind works and how humans learn. This is the beginning of his theory on multiple intelligences. This research, as it turns out, will almost single-handedly assist the beginning movement of authentic assessment. States begin to see the need to get involved in aspects of education unknown before. For example, school lunch programs in poverty zones, Head Start programs, even breakfast programs are initiated with the help of the federal government as states begin to realize the importance of funding education. The National Institute of Education becomes the U.S. Department of Education. Teachers continue to make tests suited to the content of their grade level. Tutoring programs begin to help those students who are behind the norms of the class due to disability, reading problems, behavior problems, or a variety of other recognized categories. Still, the teacher remains the critical and pivotal member of the school and classroom, and teacher-made tests prevail.

1980s   The Reagan administration attempts to abolish the Department of Education, but fails to do so. However, it issues a report called "A Nation at Risk" (1983) which begins twenty-plus years of criticism of public schooling and calls for more testing of students. Schools in the United States are compared to the Japanese schools, particularly with regard to test scores. Japan, Korea, and China outshine U.S. students in math. Pundits and politicians call for more testing. Standardized test makers seize the opportunity to make a profit and make more tests. In fact, many urban large-sized school districts begin changing their budgets to favor the purchasing of high-stakes testing in order to be eligible for more federal funds for education. This entails not only buying the test (typically made out of state), but also the costs for scoring the test, tutoring for the test, and so on. As a result, high-stakes testing becomes a huge, profit-making capitalist adventure. At the same time, the Reagan administration cuts funding for education and for educational research as money is diverted to "Star Wars" and defense budgeting. Some educa-

tors such as David Berliner and Bruce Biddle begin a close examination of data that reveal how politicians are outright wrong in their scandalous accusations against U.S. teachers, schools, and students. Following an unsuccessful attempt to thwart the publication of their text, their work is finally published as *The Manufactured Crisis* (1995). In this dreadful period for education, members of the Reagan team used their energy to try to corporatize education in the misguided attempt to prove that high-stakes testing should and would be the only standard for evaluating students and their work. While this is underway, the major teacher unions, some leading educators, and many interested parents begin to see the flaws in the Reagan proposals.

1990s   The 1990s brought assessment into prominence. The work of Grant Wiggins in particular became a beacon for educators to keep working on authentic assessment as the best method for tracking student progress, growth, and development. Teacher unions support assessment. Teachers are given professional development training to learn and incorporate methods of authentic assessment. Parents organize and voice opposition to excessive standardized and high-stakes testing. Grassroots organizations such as the nonprofit group, FAIRTEST, come alive on the Internet. FAIRTEST is an organization that collects and updates data for each state and Puerto Rico on the topics of high-stakes testing, authentic assessment, current research on the inequities of high-stakes testing, writing, textbooks, and articles on assessment. It is the watchdog of the industry, providing political and activist materials used effectively in one state and then exported as a model for other states. Many states inspired by the FAIRTEST agenda begin their own grassroots activism against testing. At the same time, politicians use superficial high-stakes testing jargon in their political campaigns. Hyper-unrealistic claims are made, such as the claim of the Goals 2000 plan that the United Sates will be the world's leader in math. (What was then known as Goals 2000 has since morphed into the flawed and

damaging law, PL. 107–110, No Child Left Behind, or NCLB legislation, see below.) The objectives of Goals 2000 have not been reached nor would they be reached by even 2005. However, educators develop authentic assessment techniques and many districts implement these techniques in addition to standardized testing. Techniques such as portfolio evaluation, to name one, become widely used in schools. State legislatures support these efforts. Districts use resources to support teachers in these efforts. The tide is turning. Wiggins and others continue publishing, retraining, and conducting workshops. Many educators document their work on assessment, and students show development and growth. Professional organizations including The National Council of Teachers of English and The National Council for the Social Studies, to name just two major organizations against high-stakes testing, issue strong statements warning against the overuse of high-stakes testing

2000–present   Attempts at authentic assessment are clearly part of the educational landscape. It even begins to take root in some southern states, traditionally states with low scores in all areas. Traditionally, the South has under-funded education. To see movement there is truly hopeful. Politically, the landscape is such that the current president favors excessive testing. However, the grassroots movement of parents, educators, administrators, and teachers, coming together to support authentic assessment is hard to stop. Even the largest professional research association in education, the American Educational Research Association, issues its firm statement against high-stakes testing. By the same token, states, one by one, are incorporating authentic assessment into curricula in their districts. Many states, such as Florida, have grassroots organizations begun by parents and teachers to monitor the excessive use of standardized testing. The Florida Coalition for Assessment Reform (FCAR, *www.fcar.org*), for example, monitors the Florida Comprehensive standardized test known as the FCAT. See the FCAR website for the studies which show that the test reduces the curricu-

lum to test preparation, harms students who have poor test-taking skills, and is biased against ethnic and racial groups to name a few of its flaws. Furthermore, FCAR has exposed the owner of the test and all its trappings, scoring, and tutoring, to be Neil Bush, the brother of Florida's governor. To his credit, Neil Bush has relinquished control of the FCAT but not his software company which is still designed to exploit the NCLB requirements. These conflict of interest issues are also examined by FCAR, and a database is available for all interested parties.

Due to a postmodern shift in thinking, it is possible to subject the high-stakes testing enshrined in NCLB to critical scrutiny, particularly in regard to the profits made by test makers as well as the socioeconomic implications of race, class, and gender issues in standardized testing. At the same time, the ground swell of grassroots activism in favor of authentic assessment continues to take shape and grow richer. In fact, one state, Iowa, refuses to participate in high-stakes testing and as a result has forfeited some types of federal money.

Another hopeful sign of the times is that universities and colleges are using authentic assessment techniques for admission, such as portfolios, over the SAT I standardized test. This development can be traced to parent, teacher, and administrator activism on behalf of students. To use just one example, many colleges of education pick up on the use of portfolios in their teacher education programs. Today's pre-service teachers are now exposed to authentic assessment, use these techniques regularly, and will be the first generation positioned to widely implement authentic assessment.

This timeline offers a lens by which to view the development of authentic assessment. It offers a way to understand the organized grassroots response to the heavy-handed corporate model which has failed so far. To help you, the reader, appreciate examples of authentic assessment, I now turn to defining what constitutes authentic assessment and focus on the example of portfolio assessment.

Some Examples of Authentic Assessment

The following are some of the most common authentic assessment techniques:

1 Performances;
2 Demonstrations;
3 Simulations;
4 Oral presentations;
5 Progress interviews;
6 Writing samples;
7 Formal observations;
8 Self-assessment;
9 Evaluations of case studies;
10 Recordings on audio or video tape of readings or performances;
11 Journal writing;
12 Writing folders chronicling a student's development through a course of study;
13 Role plays;
14 Portfolios.

For the moment, let us focus on the authentic assessment task of portfolio development. The portfolio is often the most recognized of authentic assessment techniques. Portfolio assessment is widely used to review the progress of a student's work over time. The *student* selects which artifacts go into the portfolio. For example, a student may include research papers, book reports, reflective writing, journal reflections, group work or projects, videotapes, photographs, drawings, software, slides, holograms, and even test results such as report cards. Most often there is some standard, or learning objective, which guides the student's selections for the portfolio. Again, one can see that this is a technique borrowed from artists and designers, who have always kept portfolios. In this way, the portfolio is a student's historical record. It is an information gathering process for the purpose of reflection and growth. Likewise, the portfolio uses multiple indicators and evidence sources to demonstrate a person's learning. This is a technique generated from the arts and humanities, and provides educators with the documentary progress of a stu-

dent's understanding of a given subject or knowledge base. It also places the responsibility of selecting the best work of a student on the student—where it should be. It is meant to be an active process. It is not a one-shot procedure but a *work in progress*. The portfolio is constantly changing and continually updated.

I mention portfolios here to illustrate their value as an authentic assessment. All the techniques listed above, however, share the characteristics described earlier: they require a performance and a product; they are connected to the student's world and experience; they are complex; they require multiple tasks and problem solving skills; and they provide feedback on a continual basis. The student adjusts to the feedback and performance is improved. However, if portfolios are so valuable, you may be wondering how the contents of the portfolio are in fact reviewed and assessed. Given that a **rubric** is a set of categories with a value assigned for each category by which teachers evaluate a student's work—a scoring matrix of sorts—what "rubrics" are used in the portfolio process? In what follows, I detail a rubric I use in all my classes where I ask students to do a writing assignment. This method was developed after adapting it from several rubrics and soliciting student input on its value.

Rubric

a set of scoring guidelines for evaluating students' work. Rubrics provide criteria for judgment of performance. Usually there is a scale or range of possible points assigned to a rubric. Each level of performance on the rubric must have specific descriptors that indicate what a student can do. Rubrics are often associated with standards and how those standards are met as well as authentic assessment measures. For example, if a student constructs a portfolio, the portfolio will be evaluated in terms of a rubric of some sort

Writing Rubric A: Evaluation of a Writing Rubric

Comprehensiveness and Accuracy

5 The topic is addressed creatively, thoroughly, and accurately. All pertinent information about the topic is included.

4 The topic is addressed thoroughly and accurately. All pertinent information is included.

3 The topic is addressed, but some minor information is omitted. All information is accurate.

2 The topic is addressed superficially. Important information is omitted or inaccurate.

1 The topic is addressed superficially, and so much information is inaccurate or omitted that the paper is misleading about the topic.

Conventions of Grammar and Writing

5 The organization of the paper enhances the reader's understanding of the topic, and there are no errors in grammar, punctuation, or spelling.

4 The organization of the paper is appropriate for the topic, and there are no errors in grammar, punctuation, or spelling.

3 The organization of the paper is appropriate for the topic, and there are only a few minor errors in grammar, punctuation, or spelling.

2 The organization of the paper is unclear, or there are several errors in grammar, punctuation, or spelling.

1 The organization of the paper interferes with the reader's understanding, and/or there are major errors in grammar, punctuation, and/or spelling.

Use of Sources

5 More than five sources are cited correctly in the paper and included in the reference list.

4 At least five sources are cited correctly and included in the reference list.

3 At least four sources are cited correctly and included in the reference list.

2 At least four sources are cited and included in the reference list, but their form is incorrect.

1 Fewer than four sources are cited or referenced.

Use of Appropriate Topical Examples

5 Examples appropriate to this topic are used creatively and appropriately and are explained so that the meaning of the paper is enhanced.

4 Examples are used appropriately and are explained so that they add to the meaning of the paper.

3 Examples are used, but they do not add to the meaning of the paper.

2 Examples are used but not explained.

1 Examples are used inappropriately or none are included.

The value of the rubric is that the student sees how evaluation will take place and is actually part of the evaluation insofar as the student internalizes the criteria for assessment. There are no secrets in terms of what is expected of the student. There is no subterfuge or trickery so common in standardized tests. Authentic tasks and authentic assessment provide an ethical approach to accountability.

Portfolios and Assessment

Portfolios are a key method for presenting what a student has learned. It is a multifaceted and complex product. It may have a theme and should be judged against a set of criteria usually evidenced in a given rubric. A rubric shows the viewer of the portfolio different levels of performance. Constructing portfolios and assessing them takes time, effort, and dedication to the task. Many practitioners define portfolios as a historical record of student work. It is more than a collection of papers in a folder. It is evidence of a student's work over time and may include accomplishments, capability records, a history of a person's development, and even a critique of one's work by both student and teacher. Even parents can be involved by reviewing the portfolio, giving feedback on its contents, and even rating their student's work. Of course, the items included can be many. However, whatever is included should be authentic measures of what the student learned. Usually the tasks the student performs show evidence of learning and may fall in the following major areas:

1   The tasks provide evidence of learning and growth, and sample a wide spectrum of cognitive tasks.
3   The tasks show evidence of work at different levels of understanding.
4   The tasks are tailored to the student, and allow the student to show what is known.

Similar tasks were performed in multiple ways, for a variety of purposes over time.

Thus, we see how the student is involved in the assessment process. In contrast to standardized testing, authentic assessment values the student.

Types of Portfolios

There is no one sacred model or type of portfolio. Depending on the discipline of study, for example, reading, math, physical education, art, or music, portfolio construction will vary. However, in looking over the body of literature on portfolios, there seem to be at least three types of portfolios: the "Working Portfolio," the "Record Keeping Portfolio," and the "Showcase Portfolio." A brief review of how these three major types are used is provided below.

The Working Portfolio

This type of portfolio is mostly the work of the student, accumulated on a daily basis, and gives evidence of ongoing learning in one or more areas of study. Teachers, students, and parents freely comment on all aspects of the work. The samples for the portfolio are most often selected by the student, described fully, and critiqued by the student. Teachers and parents may comment as well. However, this type of portfolio offers the student the opportunity to be self-reflective and think about the growth process itself. Many schools begin portfolios at the elementary level and carry them through to high school. One example of this is the San Diego School District which has worked on the use of portfolios for its students, and provides resources to train teachers on the use of portfolios.

The Record Keeping Portfolio

This type of portfolio may be used along with, or even integrated into, the Working Portfolio, or even the Showcase Portfolio (see below). As the name implies, it is a history of records. It may contain samples of report cards, results of tests, and other such records. It is also monitored and devised by the student with input from teachers, parents, or administrators.

The Showcase Portfolio

This is the best known and most often used type of portfolio assessment. Here, the student constructs a showcase of sample work that best demonstrates the student's progress to date in one or more areas. It is similar to the portfolio a photographer or artist might put together and usually includes completed works of high quality. It is meant to be the record of the student's best work. Thus, we see at least three types of portfolios that provide a record of authentic tasks and learning. Many states have encouraged the use of the showcase portfolio. In fact, some states now even use the portfolio in an electronic format.

The Electronic Portfolio

Portfolio assessment is well in place in most of the fifty states. In the past decade, with the growth of technology and computers in the classroom, electronic portfolios are a valuable method of assessment. Electronic portfolios allow for easier storage and retrieval of information and also permit easier inclusion of parental input and feedback. Portfolios are kept on a diskette or CD. Electronic portfolios facilitate the storing of material traditional notebook portfolios cannot accommodate. For example, songs, poetry, performances, music, and dramatic readings are more easily stored in digital form, and more accurately and visually capture the activity. Furthermore, with an electronic portfolio, a new dimension may be introduced, that of interactivity. With the powerful software available for electronic portfolios, students can be more creative and use digital means to verify and adjust their portfolio contents. Some of the current software includes ClarisWorks, Microsoft Works, HyperCard, SuperCard, and HyperStudio. Nevertheless, many question the practicality of electronic portfolios. There are multiple benefits:

1   Work can be stored digitally and more efficiently, and allows for more student flexibility. In addi-

tion, today's students take digital life as a given.

2   Digital portfolios allow for greater student mobility (e.g., when a student moves from one district to another).

3   Display of best examples may be represented more elegantly and more often with the flexibility of the digital format. Students can really show their talents.

4   Most professional organizations have already created models of electronic portfolios for social studies teachers, English teachers, math teachers, and so on.

5   Today's students often are proficient, if not experts, in computer use, and the construction of an individual electronic portfolios refines computer literacy skills.

6   Today's students spend many hours in front of a TV set or a computer screen. It seems reasonable to channel these technological interests into learning activities that stretch the student's imagination and multiple intelligences through creation of an electronic portfolio.

To cite just one example, the Wilson Academy for International Studies, San Diego Unified School District, is currently piloting a computer software application that provides for collecting, organizing, and presenting student portfolio information. This program will eventually be used by the entire district. Educators see the value of this application, and students love it, for it allows them to edit, cut, paste, and play back what they have created. Parents are delighted with the ability to take part in this activity and learn about computers and their child's work at the same time. California has supported authentic assessment and the use of electronic portfolios as evidenced by their Senate Bill 662. This bill actually mandates authentic assessment measures for all students in reading, mathematics, writing, science, and social science. Thus, the prognosis is very good for portfolio assessment, and states are getting behind educators to support these endeavors.

While teachers, parents, and students all step into

the computer age and all that it requires, one can imagine that the transition to electronic portfolios will be gradual and not necessarily easy. Nevertheless the benefits of the electronic portfolio outweigh these transitional costs. If we ask why an electronic format should be adopted, many benefits may be listed. Consider the following:

1   Electronic portfolios foster engaged learning, active learning, and student ownership of ideas. Parents also become part of the process.

2   Electronic portfolios are repositories of feedback in a medium familiar to many of today's students.

3   Electronic portfolios are the basis for student discussions of their own progress and a record of their reflections on what they learn.]

4   Electronic portfolios are easily accessible, portable, and capable of storing vast amounts of data and information.

5   Electronic portfolios can be set up to cross-reference student work in a way that is remarkable, efficient, and effective.

6   Electronic portfolios allow students to access and display evidence of multiple intelligences.

7   Electronic portfolios can teach diverse content areas and encourage creative writing.

8   Electronic portfolios can be tools for encouraging dialogue with peers and foster cross-cultural communication.

9   Electronic portfolios can use some of the energy students previously devoted to video games on actual learning and performance-based tasks.

10 Electronic portfolios can develop the multiple intelligences Howard Gardner advocates for a well rounded education.

11 Electronic portfolios have inspired many to write digital stories in the form of autobiographies, online journals, or interactive texts.

The Digital Story Explosion

One of the latest developments in electronic portfolio construction is the emergence of the digital story. A digital story is a short narrative composed online by any person who wishes to share a digital story. It is often accompanied by a video or by photographs. These stories include music, art work, narration by the writer, and, of course, any digital supplements in video or photographic format. In fact, the digital story movement is well documented on the Internet itself. The following sample highlights several key Web sites, but there are too many to list them all:

1   Center for Digital Storytelling, www.storycenter.org
2   Digitales, www.digitales.us/indewx.php
3   Third World Majority Digital Storytelling, www.cultureisaweapon.org
4   Electronic Portfolios, www.eletronicportfolios.org
5   YMDi D, www.ymdi.org

Each of these Web sites provides the student with a description of digital storytelling, various examples of existing digital stories for portfolios, and invites the student to take part in digital storytelling. One can even find a handbook on the Electronic Portfolios site for creating electronic portfolios. Many professionals offer their own work as samples for study and reflection. It is clear that the electronic portfolio and the digital story are two examples of the next generation of authentic assessment. The possibilities are endless.

Portfolio Contents

The creative activity of constructing a portfolio rests on the student and thus is a true authentic performance-based activity. Any system may be used. For example, some portfolios are displayed in binders, boxes, display cases, or some combination. Currently, electronic portfolios on disk or CD are used in some schools. Whatever method of display is used, reason dictates that it should be manageable, accessible, and portable. Samples are created, selected, and self-evaluated by the student. The contents of the portfolio may include:

1   "Works in Progress," such as writing samples in various drafts and revisions, that show evidence of learning;

2   "Outstanding Products," such as poetry, short stories, photographs, artwork, description of activities, audiotapes, videotapes, CDs, book reports, math problem-solving work, and so on;

3   "Evaluative Comments" by the student, teacher, or parent;

4   "Digital Stories" by the student and evaluator.

Remember that the portfolio is the culmination of an extended process. Prior to the construction of student portfolios, teachers already have a series of goals, plans, and objectives for students that enable them to take charge of their learning. Teachers work to make each activity relevant and meaningful to the student, focusing on complex skills. In other words, portfolios are living records of the authentic tasks students have performed and critiqued. Portfolios widen the repertoire of assessment strategies and provide solid evidence that students can *do* something. It is a testament to what the student has accomplished and learned. Thus, portfolios are a critical element in the process of assessment. Addition information and key research and writing on portfolios can be found at the following organizations and their associated Web sites:

Files available at the Coalition of Essential Schools:

Coalition of Essential Schools: Welcome
http://www.essentialschools.org
    The main home page for the Coalition of Essential Schools: The Digital Portfolio: A Richer Picture of Student Performance
http://www.essentialschools.org/pubs/exhib_schdes/dp/dpframe.htm
The HTML version of an excellent CD produced by David Niguidula on the research in five different schools:

Technology in the Essential School: Making Change in the Information Age
http://www.essentialschools.org/pubs/horace/10/v10n03.html
Horace: vol. 10, no. 3
Demonstrating Student Performance in Essential Schools

Show, Don't Tell: Video and Accountability:
http://www.essentialschools.org/cs/resources/view/ces_res/229

A research paper on the use of video and accountability: The Digital Portfolio: A Richer Picture of Student Performance
http://www.essentialschools.org/cs/resources/view/ces_res/225

A research paper on the Coalition's design of a digital portfolio under development at several schools: The New York Assessment Collection Web Version: Table of Contents
http://www.essentialschools.org/pubs/exhib_schdes/nyac_web/toc.htm

Portfolio Assessment Example

Reproduced below is one way to assess a sample for a portfolio entry as suggested by Silver, Strong, and Perini (2000). Imagine this for a verbal-linguistic assessment menu:

Mastery = The ability to use language to describe events and sequence activities

a   Write an article.
b   Develop a plan.
c   Put together a magazine.
d   Develop an newscast.
e   Describe a complex procedure.

Interpersonal Ability = The ability to use language to build trust and rapport

a   Write a letter.

b   Make a pitch.

c   Conduct an interview.

Understanding = The ability to develop logical arguments and use rhetoric

a   Make a case.

b   Make or defend a decision.

c   Advance a theory.

d   Interpret a text.

Self-Expressive Ability = The ability to use metaphoric and expressive language

a   Develop a plan to direct.

b   Tell a story.

c   Develop an advertising campaign.

This is only one example of a matrix for assessing a sample in a student's portfolio. It is not surprising that portfolio assessment is a richer, more complex alternative to the typical one-shot, commercial standardized high-stakes test. Portfolio creation is an authentic task that anyone can learn to do well, and the art of journal writing is too. Let us turn to journal writing to illustrate its value as an important component of an authentic assessment task.

Journal Writing as an Authentic Assessment Task

Students and colleagues have often asked me why one should invest time in journal writing. Journal writing allows us to reflect upon the experiences and events in our lives, as well as our beliefs and behaviors. The act of writing down our thoughts allows us to step into our inner mind and to interpret our behaviors, experiences, and beliefs. As an element of authentic assessment, journal writing allows the student to explore content area at any level by writing out reflections, ideas, and so on. It can be done as part of a hard text or an electronic portfolio, and it stands as a continual feedback technique so important to authentic assessment.

For example, a student conducting a miniature study in a qualitative methods class wrote in her jour-

nal and described some of her inner thoughts:

> I am a bit wary of this research. . . . Am I really a researcher because I am taking a class? Can I ever hope to portray what someone else believes or at least says she believes? How will I know if I am being fair? Will I be able to trust this person? Will she trust me? Why should she trust me? Am I being too critical of myself? I am waiting here and she is already 20 minutes late. I hope she gets here soon. . . . Here she comes. Now I try to capture this person's thoughts on why she is an administrator.

As we look at this journal entry, we can see the student/researcher in training, asking questions that prompt reflection on various issues about the research process. She is beginning to know more about herself and her strengths and weaknesses. Journal writing is perhaps the most accessible authentic performance task available to students and teachers.

Journal writing has a long and reliable history in the arts and humanities, as well as in the sciences. It is not by accident that artists, writers, dancers, musicians, physicians, poets, architects, saints, scientists, therapists, and educators use journal writing in their lives. Virtually in every field, greatness is often accompanied by detailed and lengthy journals. Journal writing should be viewed as a powerful heuristic tool and classroom research technique. Keeping a classroom journal helps to illuminate and refine thinking skills at all levels. In addition, keeping a journal is an interactive tool of communication between the teacher, quite possibly the parent, and the student. Journal writing also allows for multiple intelligences to be displayed, for it is not limited to the written word.

In his text *A Book of One's Own: People and Their Diaries* (1995), Thomas Mallon has come up with several categories of journal writers, types of writers who exemplify different intelligences. In his overview of diarists and journal writers, he categorizes writers as follows:

1   Chroniclers: People who keep their diaries every single day as if recording the news.

2 Travelers: People who keep a written record during a special time, such as a vacation or a trip.
3 Pilgrims: People who want to discover who they really are.
4 Creators: People who write to sketch out ideas and inventions in art or science.
5 Apologists: People who write to justify something they have done to plead their case before all who read the journal.
6 Confessors: People who direct ritual confessions, conducted with the promise of secrecy or anonymity.
7 Prisoners: People who must live their lives in prisons or who may be incapacitated in one way or another and as a result live their own lives vicariously by keeping a journal.

Of course, any writer might be a combination of any of these categories, but these distinctions can be useful as a tool to understand different approaches to keeping a journal. Mallon gives numerous examples of individuals who fall into these categories to illustrate the importance of keeping a journal. In fact, he became interested in writing his book because he himself had kept a journal for over thirty years.

Currently, there are many wonderful resources on journal writing in popular culture, and many are specifically accessible through the Internet. In a recent search of "journal writing" on the Internet, I noticed there were over three million entries. In fact, there is even a journal-writing course on the Internet offered by a group called Via Creativa, and many Web sites are devoted to the journal writing method of Ira Progoff (1992)—journal writing as a tool for therapy and spiritual growth.

Journal writing may also include drawings, art work, and combinations of visual, spatial, mathematical, and verbal intelligences. Having reviewed portfolio development and journal writing, let us now turn to the context for these types of authentic tasks.

Authentic Assessment in Today's World

The politics of schooling most often gets in the way of student progress. Bureaucrats want a score in most cases. They want to measure progress of students with a one-shot score because it is easy, it requires less time, and, as they say, time is money. In the past, educators, researchers, and writers did not question typical tests. However, with the social movements of the 1960s onward, many sectors of society began questioning civil rights, women's rights, gay rights, and so on. When people became concerned with issues of equality at the macro level, it did not take long until this discussion trickled down to the micro level of the schoolroom. On a global level, people were asking for fairness. Authentic assessment is a fair, balanced, and ethical process. Recall that there is no subterfuge or trickery in authentic assessment because the student is aware of all expectations for performance.

In the schools, demands for fairness were applied to the most basic objective of teaching: how we assess what students know. It takes much more time, effort, involvement, teacher training, and teacher professional development to put authentic assessment techniques into practice. Over the past twenty years, educators in every state have been clamoring to know more about authentic assessment. Why? Put simply, because it makes sense. Ask yourself, would you want your child judged and graded by a one-shot test, which provides a simple score, or would you rather have your child assessed and graded by performance-tasks that show not only what your child has learned, but also what your child can do? The reasons for preferring authentic assessment are the following:

1   Authentic assessment is fair. No one racial or ethnic group is penalized as is often the case with a one-shot standardized test score.
2   Authentic assessment tells us a great deal about how students connect content knowledge with a given problem under study in the student's world. Making connections can be distorted or

truncated in typical testing.

3 Authentic assessment provides feedback on a student's progress on a continual basis. Typical testing involves a one-shot torpedo approach to progress.

4 Authentic assessment shows how a student constructs a product or performance so that the student's growth as well as the thought processes of the student can be seen. The responsibility is on the student to describe, explain, and make connections to the real work in any given project.

5 Authentic assessment overall provides for continual feedback, allowing the student to adjust and improve performance. In the real world, this is how we get on in life. We continually redirect our efforts based on feedback. Does this not make more sense than any one-shot test score for understanding progress?

These are not the only reasons to select authentic assessment as a solid evaluative technique. Obviously, in today's world, students are bombarded with media images and information technology, and one might say, a sophisticated information explosion. The needs of today's student are demanding and competitive. Therefore, it is necessary to give students the opportunity to display what they have learned through performance-based authentic assessment and actual products that verify a student's progress.

How Authentic Assessment Is Suited for Today's World

The pace, complexity, and demands of today's world require much from student learning. Oddly enough, it was years ago, at the beginning of the twentieth century that John Dewey made similar assertions. Dewey is known as America's foremost philosopher of education. He wrote prolifically on the topic of experience and education. He reasoned that students must have actual experience with learning something or its meaning would be lost. For example, rather than read about how to bake a cake, a student should actually perform the activity of baking a cake. The preparation of material and ingredients, the putting together of the ingredients, baking, frosting, decorating, and so on, all are part of the actual real-world experience of the student. At the time Dewey was writing he encountered mixed reviews. Educators were both intrigued and enthused by his work. However, he worked in the realm of philosophy applied to the real world of education, earning him the title of pragmatist. He once said there is nothing so practical as a good theory. With an understanding of Dewey's work in experience and education, I see Dewey as the starting point for what we now call authentic assessment. It is important to understand our history, in order to understand where we are now and where we are going. American Pragmatism, the philosophy most often associated with John Dewey, provides us with the first seeds of what we now call authentic assessment. Put simply, experience is one of the greatest teachers, if not the single greatest teacher. Authentic assessment requires the student to experience what is being learned, whether it is baking a cake or documenting a semester's work of writing assignments.

Learning from the Research and Writing on Assessment

In attempting to define and describe authentic assessment, all previous knowledge of typical, standardized, large-scale testing needs to be put aside. To phrase it simply, typical, standardized, large-scale tests do not prepare students for the real world. They do not prepare students for what to *do* with knowledge. Assessment, on the other hand, is about *doing*. Students *create* a product or *perform* an act. They must *enact* their knowledge. Would we judge a lawyer merely on her knowledge of torts class, or would we also judge her on her performance in a real courtroom? Would we judge the ballet dancer on floor exercises only in class or also on live performances of the ballet "Swan Lake" to test knowledge of ballet? In other words, we need to assess the student's

knowledge of how to actually prepare for the various roles and opportunities that are encountered in the real world of work, study, and play. Knowledge is not all clean cut and easily catalogued. It is "messy" and uneven out there in the real world. If the student is to succeed, the student must be able to *do* the subject. The medical student who becomes a surgeon will be assessed on surgery, not just knowledge of anatomy. Stop for a moment and think about your own schooling and your own learning experiences. When you learned something in geography class, for example, did you memorize some facts for a specific test? Did you then receive a grade for this? Can you now recall those facts? These are rhetorical questions, but let's face it, most of us went to schools where this behavior was the norm. To further pursue the geography example, an authentic assessment practitioner would approach it in a different way. She would first decide what was critical to know about the geography unit under study, and then design authentic performance tasks to see what the student can do with the information. For example, look at the breakdown of the study on page 47.

The research and writing on assessment clearly indicates that there is a tension between authentic assessment and one-shot, large-scale testing. On the one hand, authentic assessment tasks are designed to find out what students know and what they can actually do with their knowledge. On the other hand, the generic testing approach requires a student to memorize facts, out of the context of the learning situation, and does not require a check on what a student can do. Authentic assessment tasks are designed to focus on both understanding and application. Thus, students use judgment and strive for competence and mastery of subject matter. With this in mind, let's examine some major themes in the assessment literature by looking at some of the key writers and research on authentic assessment. This approach will help clarify the tremendous interest, on the part of educators, in the assessment movement.

CONTRASTING APPROACHES TO TESTING

Typical Geography Test	**Authentic Assessment**
1 Requires *memorization* of the capitals of all Asian countries.	1 Requires knowledge of *trends* and *changes* in politics and society in the major geographic regions of Asia.
2 Requires a written test on the capitals.	2 Requires a series of projects which might include interviewing a person from Asia, writing a play about a particular series of events in an Asian country, scanning the newspaper for reports on Asia, or uses a journal to document thoughts, reflections, and ideas about articles or books read about Asia. Alternatively, students select an Asian country, say Indonesia, and plan a three-week itinerary for a visit to Indonesia, naming key sites and documenting their history as they develop a budget for such a trip and integrate all the facts in a way that demonstrates the student's knowledge about Indonesia in particular and Asia in general.

Theme One: The Value and Importance of Assessment

The development and application of authentic assessment in various disciplines or areas of study leads us to see the value and importance of assessment. Lund (1997) has written in the area of physical education and authentic assessment. Lund asks us to think about the lifeguard at the pool. How did the lifeguard achieve competence? Of course, the lifeguard had some classroom work in terms of reading, writing, and reflection. Beyond that, the lifeguard had further tests. These tests allowed the lifeguard to demonstrate, for example, how to rescue a drowning victim. There were levels of circumstances "surrounding the drowning." Yes, the drowning scenarios were simulations of actual possible drownings, but the prospective lifeguard was testing on solving these problems as if they were actual events.

Simulations can be used as an authentic assessment technique. The student had to show competence against a set of criteria for each of several possible drowning scenarios. Lund points out that authentic assessment is becoming more popular and useful among educators as they seek to prepare students for life after graduation. Students must demonstrate a thoughtful understanding of all their book knowledge, so to speak. Mastery involves more than recall for a test. Using the lifeguard example, a written test cannot possibly tell the teacher if the student is able to rescue a drowning victim. The student has to demonstrate the ability to do it. This approach reiterates Grant Wiggins's main ideas about authentic assessment: Authentic assessment tasks are set in a meaningful context allowing the student to make connections between real world experiences and school-based ideas. In the process, authentic assessments focus on higher-level thinking, problem solving, and more complex levels of learning.

In addition to books, Wiggins also has written numerous articles on authentic assessment. I have selected three of his most powerful articles (1989, 1993a, 1993b) for specific consideration. Wiggins (1993b) explains why it is futile to try to teach everything of value to students by the time they leave high school. Rather, he argues, we should instill in students a deep love for learning, a burning desire to question and keep questioning throughout their lives. This observation, of course, resonates with the writings of John Dewey. Wiggins points out that the current rush of books on what every student should know in grades x, y, and z, oddly enough, never explores *why* students don't know where Mexico is on the map or when the Civil War was fought. He claims that for every student who may not know the exact years of the Civil War, somewhere out there, there is a well-educated adult who also is unaware of this fact and likely does not deem it very important. Wiggins further points out that quite often teaching is reduced to the written equivalent of TV news sound bites or entertainment. One of the reasons for this crowding is the fact that many groups lobby hard for their ideas to be taught. However, the problem, he points out, is that the subject matter may indeed be taught, but it is not *learned*. According to Wiggins, the problem with student ignorance is really the problem of *adult ignorance* as to how thoughtful and long-lasting understanding is achieved. On the one hand, trying to teach everything of importance in a limited amount of time reduces education to a series of forgettable "fact trivia" and "sound bites." On the other hand, selectively choosing subjects forces schooling to be a necessarily inadequate apprenticeship. This is the "breadth versus depth" dilemma at the heart of curriculum and instruction.

Wiggins advises that students must be enabled to know and learn about their own ignorance, gain control over the resources available for making progress and then take pleasure in lifelong learning. An authentic education, then, would be one of developing the "habits" of mind and "high standards of craftsmanship," given the reality of one's own ignorance. Thus, this view stands in contrast to the prevailing view that the more we know, the more we should test in order to show what we can recall for those typical tests.

Another, even more powerful piece (Wiggins 1993), develops this argument regarding the use of judgment in context. According to Wiggins, real learning takes place when students use judgment to complete an authentic task so as to show their level of understanding of a given subject. He begins with the question "what is performance?" This question is critical for Wiggins. He differentiates between drilled skills and performance by use of a soccer game example. In soccer, and many other sports, practice drills are the beginning of every practice session. However, if a student practices only these drills, can we say that the student knows how to perform in a game of soccer? The drills in soccer are very much like the test items on the typical test. All the drills together, though, are never equal to the actual performance test, the actual soccer game. Earlier I used the example from dance. The ballet dancer in train-

ing begins with numerous drills at the bar, followed by floor exercises, and then combinations of two or three steps put together. The real test, however, is an actual choreographed performance of a ballet. It is important, then, to ask ourselves what the equivalent of the ballet performance, or the soccer game, is for our academic subjects. Wiggins goes further and leaves us to question whether we really want to myopically focus on test scores. Should we want to look ahead toward the intellectual horizon of life long learning?

The third important research article documents Wiggins's (1993a) work on new schools and new communities. This periodical piece is about "embracing accountability." He basically argues that no teacher can be successful unless the teacher is held accountable. To be held accountable means simply to be responsible for one's work. In fact, he goes so far as to say any hope of ever achieving teacher excellence depends on accountability. He has an involved argument about the importance of feedback for both student and teacher. He argues against the view that teaching is merely "teaching to the test." He passionately argues for building a performance appraisal system. He reminds us that the purpose of assessment is to *improve* performance, not just *audit* performance. This is a must for those seriously trying to understand the value of assessment. Standardized tests take only a static "snap shot" of student learning. Authentic assessment, on the other hand, is designed to improve performance.

Theme Two: Sample Alternatives to High-Stakes Testing

The reader may find different examples of authentic assessment in various disciplines and fields in journals, books, and on the Internet. Although there are numerous examples, I have selected the following. The fields that most often use authentic assessment include physical education, the arts, and the humanities. Our first example is from the area of literature in the classroom. Walker (1997) writes of creating a

new course to integrate writing, speaking, listening, reading, and literature. She describes a literature class she taught in Native American and colonial literature for high school students in the eleventh grade. For assessment, she used a research project as a performance assessment. Students worked in groups to study Native American tribes. Students studied migration, ancestors, and the culture. Students used formats such as game shows, panel discussions, interviews, and skits to convey what they learned. Next, students created a newspaper on the literature of that period and a thematic mobile, each part of which had a thematic quotation from writers of the period. For the final exam, students had to create a timeline depicting the trends in literature during the colonial period. The overall effect was active, engaged learning. Students had to demonstrate what they learned in written, verbal, and artistic forms—an authentic assessment. They were all able to justify their work, critique their work, and chart their own growth, development, and progress.

Another example of an authentic assessment of writing is evidenced by the rubric I often use when I ask students to write an autobiographical narrative describing how they came into the field of education. Students at the university level tend to write about personal experiences with a teacher in their past. Autobiography is a particular literary genre, yet it can be assessed for form, content, and style. Here is the rubric I created based on experience, trial and error, and common sense.

Rubric for Evaluating Writing

Project: Autobiography

a   Chronological facts and figures: Students must report a chronology of events of their own choosing which describes their own characteristics of race, class, gender, ethnic origins, and schooling.

b   Use of supporting sources: Students need to find supporting literature to indicate their aware-

ness of the categories race, class, gender, ethnicity, and schooling in the literature and connect this information to their own situation.

c Recognition of themes: Students are asked to identify at least two recurring themes in their autobiographical account.

d Summary of themes, indicators, and meaning: Students are asked to construct a solid summary of the themes, indicators, and meaning in their essay.

These four categories are assessed in the following scale:

4 = Element is consistently demonstrated.
3 = Element is frequently demonstrated.
2 = Element is occasionally demonstrated.
1 = Element is not demonstrated.

Still another type of authentic assessment technique I use is that of the *critical case study.* I ask my students to create a critical case study of a major problem they have come across in their own classrooms or workplace. Because most of my students are educators or potential educators, this is easy for them to do. Then they must critique the problem from the standpoint of at least two theorists, identify how they would approach the problem in the real world, and then attempt to create a case study on the matter. The students create and construct case scenarios offering various solutions to their own day-to-day problems from their own lives. They seek feedback from each other and then redirect their own writing and cases. Thus, they have a feedback loop which allows for even more growth, change, and development. The analysis they complete must be one which they fully describe and explain based on solving the problem named. Students understand that their autobiography is a work in progress and they may adjust their writing at any time. All this work then is placed in an ongoing portfolio of learning for which the student has responsibility.

Summary

In summary, we have seen examples of applied authentic assessment techniques at several grade levels, reviewed a brief history of authentic assessment, and analyzed the context for assessment. The many Internet and hard text resources listed in Chapter Five of this text are meant to be a starting point for understanding assessment in today's world. In Chapter Two, we go more deeply into examples of authentic assessment, standards, their inherent problems, and the need for critical thinking as a goal for authentic assessment.

GLOSSARY

Authentic assessment—requires authentic tasks that show students' abilities. Students receive feedback and redirection to allow for their growth; students have a part in the process and outcome

High-stakes testing—standardized tests whose results are used as the basis of important decisions, such as decreasing a school's funding or retaining a student in a grade level

Multiple intelligences—a theory formulated by Howard Gardner, according which the concept of intelligence includes musical, bodily-kiesthetic, locigal-mathematical, spatial, interpersonal, intrapersonal, and linguistic forms of intelligence

No Child Left Behind Act (NCLB)—This law began as PL 107–110, signed by George W. Bush in his first term as President and is a permutation of the annual Elementary and Secondary Education Act. The Act basically requires Adequate Yearly Progress (AYP) on state tests in major subjects every year. It remains highly controversial because it has neither been meeting its stated purpose by just about any measure nor has it taken account of research on child development, research on learning, and research on testing. It has the goal that, by the year 2014, all schools in all states will be performing at levels required by the federal government

Performance-based assessment—this term is often used interchangeably with authentic assessment. It is assessment based on performance tasks designed to show what a student can do, such as making a movie, performing a dance, writing an essay, constructing art work, preparing demon-

strations, sharing journal writing, or conducting an interview

Rubric—a set of scoring guidelines for evaluating students' work. Rubrics provide criteria for judgment of performance. Usually there is a scale or range of possible points assigned to a rubric. Each level of performance on the rubric must have specific descriptors that indicate what a student can do. Rubrics are often associated with standards and how those standards are met as well as authentic assessment measures. For example, if a student constructs a portfolio, the portfolio will be evaluated in terms of a rubric of some sort

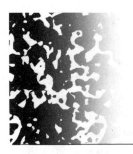

CHAPTER TWO

Standards, Assessment, and Critical Thinking

Mediocrity is going to kill us a lot sooner than any bombs, enemies, or weapons.

Anonymous

In order to really get to the heart of authentic assessment, we must spend some time trying to figure out the standards movement and its connection to high-stakes testing. In addition, we need to talk about what kinds of students we want: students who can memorize and repeat disconnected facts or students who are critical thinkers. I am writing this primer in part to argue that we would be better served as a society if we allowed our students to take responsibility for their learning, as Dewey suggested. Students able to exercise critical thinking skills can tap into a world of creativity, imagination, and the arts and make connections to their own lives. Let's take a look at the standards movement, and what we know about its persistent problems.

Understanding the Standards Movement

A challenging question we might put to ourselves is how to get students to assess themselves using critical thinking as an alternative to high-stakes testing. This does not mean we would give up responsibility, accountability, or any personal investment in learning. In fact, it would expand our repertoire of ways to look at schooling that is more meaningful and even more useful. In order to fully understand authentic assessment, we need to include some discussion of standards. I want to begin this discussion with the notion that we are at an exciting moment in our history in terms of deciding on the importance of critical thinking as it relates to assessment and standards. If we look at the root of the words *standards* and *critical* we have a good beginning for understanding. The word *standards* comes from the idea of a rallying point or yardstick. The word *critical* is from the Greek "kritikos" meaning discerning judgment. One could also apply the word "kriterion" or standard here. Let me explain by looking back at the history of the standards movement, in order to deal with these questions. The standards movement is often linked to the educational reform movement sparked by the report "A Nation at Risk." Educational reform, though, has a longer history in America. Oddly enough, in the "A Nation at Risk" report—which has now been debunked as mostly hearsay and evidentially poor—its authors claimed that a rising tide of mediocrity would flood us all. However, the mediocrity these authors report is more the result of misguided high-stakes testing and standards rather than a genuine reflection of student achievement or student potential. Nevertheless, all the buzz words such as "whole language," "technology reform," "school within a school," "math their way," and so on still resonate. In fact, both individual educators and professional organizations have recently demanded standards as a remedy to almost every educational problem. Even my doctoral students who are now teachers often remark that current reforms are usually politically inspired and always revolve around

"getting those test scores higher and higher" on pain of appearing in the morning newspaper as a "lower scoring school." More specifically, many states, e.g., Florida and Illinois, are currently threatening to remove funds or actually have removed funds from lower scoring schools altogether. Both of these results can cause children in these schools to internalize these "lower" ratings. Worse, control of education has shifted from local to state and national levels. I cannot stress strongly enough how this is doomed to failure. The history of education in the United States is a history of local control. In order to develop a critical thinking approach to standards and assessment, we need to begin challenging prevailing policies that work against the critical thinking approach. Testing and publishing test scores will not cause many people to become critical thinkers. Rote, repetition, and recall are the bottom of the cognitive barrel. How can we hope to tap into students' critical thinking and higher-order skills at the lowest level of thinking?

The time has come to respond to critics who say that critical thinking skills themselves should have standards. Critical thinking, though, is inherently critical: Critical thinkers continually assess their own progress and continue to raise standards for themselves. They see standards as dynamic, in process, and continually renewed due to consistent and continual feedback in the learning loop. What might standards really look like for critical thinking? At the very least, we would have to include something like this:

1   Students and teachers determine the extent of information needed;
2   Students access this information effectively;
3   Students evaluate information and sources critically;
4   Students incorporate selected information into their knowledge base;
5   Students understand the complexity of a given topic area;
6   Students are active in redirecting knowledge to create new knowledge;

7   Students continue to raise the bar in terms of personal growth, and use of their imagination and creativity.

If we take a developmental view of standards, students first use a set of foundational skills and then move onto higher-order thinking skills. When I talk about critical thinking, I refer to the seminal text by Richard Paul, *Critical Thinking: How to Prepare Students for a Rapidly Changing World* (1993). It is almost impossible to discuss critical thinking without talking about authentic assessment. Authentic assessment is an approach that allows students to show what they can *do*. Authentic assessment is inevitable if one takes a critical approach. Authentic assessment is the antidote to excessive, high-stakes standardized testing. Moreover, ethical questions can be seriously addressed by students and teachers when using authentic assessment techniques. Imbedded in the standards and assessment movements are ethical issues which have long been dismissed by proponents of high-stakes standardized testing.

Ethical Problems with the Standards Movement

When thinking about the standards movement, the following questions can help to frame the issues:

1   Who benefits from setting standards?
2   Why the veil of secrecy surrounding testing which is at odds with the value of fairness and openness in a democratic society?
3   Whose voice is taken into account when the standards are formulated?
4   Are we creating new inequalities by advocating standards?
5   Are we really going to label most schools as failures?
6   Can we just look away from the increasing number of minority students who are dropping out of school, especially in states such as Texas?
7   Are the high-stakes tests worthwhile in the first place?
8   Connecting standards to high-stakes testing

and the mass production of textbooks only offers one type of thinking and learning. Do we really want a one-size-fits-all policy?

9   Can we as a nation afford to allow bureaucrats and businessmen to dictate the way tests and standards are used at the local level?

10 Is there really any evidence for a "crisis" in education?

11 What role do the media play in their refusal to report the facts on these matters?

As can be seen, the problems created by standards are complex. Let's look at the first problem: Who benefits from setting standards? The extremely high monetary cost of the tests themselves, the upkeep of all the prep materials, scoring, coding, and the veil of secrecy, e.g., indicate the very high cost of standardized testing. Often, as in the case of Florida, there is a conflict of interest if the owner of the test is politically connected. Clearly, *the testing industry benefits from encouraging testing.* In addition, as those of us with a career in education realize, testing is often handled questionably. Some educational leaders argue that some teachers actually teach to the test alone, thereby casting teaching as mere test preparation. So while the standards movement was initiated with grandiose aims and world-class standards, in actual cases standards have become distorted by politics and expedience. With an all-out emphasis on testing and standards, there is little time for critical thinking activities and the actual content of the curriculum.

The Texas School Reform Case

Take Texas, for example. Texas illustrates some of the political and economic consequences of the push for standards. The well-known researcher, Linda McNeil (2000), has presented a thorough analysis of the reform movement in Texas from the mid-1980s to the present in her book *Contradictions of School Reform.* She completed her study to document and track standardized reforms from their beginnings in the state legislature to their effects on

the curriculum in schools, teachers, and student achievement. The "reform" in Texas was begun by Ross Perot which basically took local control of schools away from the public and professional teachers, and gave it to private businesses controlled external management and external accountability systems. This major shift from public to private is an underlying but barely examined reality. The accountability system in Texas was previously called the Texas Assessment of Academic Skills or TAAS. However, due to many studies which unmasked the weaknesses in this testing system, the test was renamed the Texas Assessment of Knowledge and Skills or TAKS, as if renaming a problem would resolve it. TAKS was first administered in the 2002–2003 school year.

In order to understand the history of Texas standards and standardized assessment generally, TAAS and the reasons why it failed need to be understood. TAAS was promoted for the following reasons:

1　It had improved the schools;
2　Teachers and principals were held accountable for test scores;
3　"Performance contracts" were used for evaluating principals based on test scores; and
4　Test results were used for decisions about school practice.

Mr. Perot was very articulate about how to improve schools through testing and basically argued "if it's good enough for business it's good enough for schools." The injection of a business model, along with the usual politics, complicated matters even further. McNeil (2000), however, looks closely at this situation and points out the flaws in this approach to education.

For one thing, McNeil raises the issues of historical inequities in funding schools, staff allocation, investment in materials, and support from the broader community. In fact, many observers believe that what drives the standards movement in general can be distilled into two assumptions, both based on fear:

1   Our nation is *losing its competitive edge* and is falling behind other countries. In order to compete in the global marketplace, we must push students to learn more and learn faster. We can do this by raising standards.

2   If we *raise standards for all students,* we automatically address the disparity between high and low achievers thus diminishing some of the fear of not competing in the global work force.

Today we must listen to test makers arguing that the best way to resolve these inequities is through standardized testing. By raising standards and using appropriate tests to measure achievement, we automatically improve education and our place in a competitive global economy. If only it were that simple. If only they understood how John Dewey argued for a child-centered, critical thinking approach to education rather than a test-centered curriculum in the attempt to address inequality.

McNeil also reports on various teacher reactions and changed behavior when a mandated curriculum driven by testing is enforced. Teachers basically complained that the TAAS prep component of the curriculum totally recast the role of teachers and principals. Teachers were silenced and marginalized. They had little voice in the matter and so did principals. However, what is the cost of standardization and compliance? Where is the space for the "public" in "public schools"? As standardization is increased, will we eliminate the voice of parents, teachers, and other community members? Similarly, who really benefits most from all the noise about raising standards? In the highly politicized milieu of an election year, politicians especially love the opportunity to get tough with standards yet provide less in terms of resources. Does that make any sense?

McNeil also points out that mandatory state tests have effectively become an instrument by which to implement state standards. By aggregating test scores, the inequity within and between schools is masked. For example, a suburban school may do well in preparing college bound students. At the

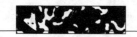

same time they may not do well at all in preparing non-college bound students. Furthermore, by aggregating all the scores, someone looking at the test data may see the school as uniformly responsible for all its students. *Thus, the way data are reported is a serious problem and has political, racial, and economic overtones.* In addition, many ethical issues arise, most notably the issue of the time spent on test prep rather than actual class work and content mastery.

Teaching to the Test and Other Maladies

In Texas, McNeil (2000) reported that many of the schools she studied consumed large amounts of time practicing for tests. Students practiced "bubbling" in answers and learned to recognize that test makers never have the same letter choice for a correct answer three times in a row. In fact, to help students remember this, a catchy phrase was repeated: "Three in a row, no, no, no!" What are we to make of this? Still further, principals who participated in the study reported using the lion's share of the budget to purchase expensive study materials. Again, we return to the question, who benefits from all this? Do children benefit from all this testing or do test makers? What would the state of the art look like if we were to implement standards for critical thinking or at least incorporate into testing and into the written standards a space for emphasizing critical thinking activities such as journal writing, reflective essays, and critical reasoning? What this Texas case shows us is that teaching toward tests alone diminishes students' ability to practice critical thinking skills. Do we really want to go that route?

Other writers have also come together and identified the case of Texas as illustrative of the dismal results teaching to the test at the expense of the original and actual curriculum produces. In their book *American Standards* (2001), Horn and Kincheloe have documented how activist parents sued Texas for spending time preparing students for tests rather than preparing them for life. In fact, they highlight the larger issues raised by the Texas case, including:

1   *The acceptance of the "efficiency technical rational" model.* This problem is best understood by the efforts to make teachers good floor managers of little student workers. With prepackaged teaching recipes or worse, teaching to the test, teachers are no longer public intellectuals in charge of their craft. In addition, key questions about education, such as what to teach and how to teach it, are outright dismissed. In Texas, when educators fell into the techno-rational trap, they avoided dealing with the rigor of academic excellence. After all, it is much easier to go for the one-shot standardized test.

2   *Fragmentation and reduction of the curriculum.* Teachers operate in a complex world. They know about individual differences, and how children grow, develop, and learn. By reducing the curriculum to excessive reliance on standardized test scores, a great disservice, if not harm, is done to children who have special needs, diverse backgrounds, speak English as a second or third language, etc. In fact, in the case against the Texas Education Agency (*GI Forum v. TEA 2000*), the plaintiff's summary included some powerful testimony regarding the TAAS exit test: The TAAS exit test wreaks havoc with the educational opportunities of the state's African American and Hispanic students. The results of the test show that minorities consistently score lower than whites, an indication that surely something was wrong with the test. Unfortunately, the court sided with the state of Texas rather than the coalition suing Texas, effectively upholding states' rights over students' rights. Apparently, complexity and ambiguity have no place in Texas.

Multiple-choice tests

multiple-choice tests usually have many test items. For each question, the test taker selects one answer from a given list of four or more choices. Most standardized tests are made up of multiple-choice items

3   *Dumbing everyone down via standards, tests, and so on.* Because the test drives everything in the schools, all other parts of schooling are left out. As a result, the students who end up graduating are either simply good at taking tests or naively satisfied with practicing answers to **multiple-choice tests**. Perhaps the greatest mistake is

that because so much energy goes into testing, the actual rigor of scholarship and content knowledge is overlooked. This emphasis on test results gives students, teachers, and educators a false sense of learning.

4 *Standards as part of a right wing reeducation project.* The powerholders in Texas were a group of far-right ideologues, yet claimed to be neutral. In a way, the Texas case represented a right-wing reaction to the advancements of the civil, feminist, and gay rights movements. The far religious right wants to take back the education system to a time when their agenda was the status quo. However, to deny diversity in American society makes no sense. A one-size-fits-all approach has never worked in the past, and certainly does not work in the present.

5 *Standards as part of resurgent white supremacy.* Ray Horn (2001) has studied the Texas case and what the TAAS system was really all about. His investigations have exposed the racist nature of the TAAS, and the evidence is overwhelming. Not only do minorities fare worse, as multiple studies have shown, but in order to not be labeled as racist, Texas personnel have simply exempted those students who continue to do poorly on the tests. They have tried to manage the social world in a way that will avoid controversy based on results of the tests. Worse, Texas does not account for those students who drop out of high school prior to the test. Such students do not get counted as dropouts and are entirely forgotten. In other words, of the many Hispanic and African American dropouts in Texas, most are unreported in the formal rolls. Furthermore, current lawsuits against the Texas Education Agency claim that Texas is single-handedly depriving minority students of an equal educational opportunity.

6 *The need for a social vision guided by professional educators, not corporate accountants.* Shamefully, the corporate model has side-lined professional educators from working out a strong vision and

philosophy of education for young people of all cultures. What we learn from the Texas case is how rampant educational racism is in the United States.

Obviously Texas is not the only state with these problems. I use the Texas case because it has been researched very carefully and numerous books, Web sites, and articles have exposed its problems. My hope is that we can learn from history rather than repeat the mistakes already revealed through the Texas case. Though many lawsuits against the Texas Education Agency are still pending—and may take decades to resolve—while we wait, surely we should call upon our best ideas to solve some of these self-created problems.

Alternatives to Teaching to the Test

Critical thinking techniques offer an alternative to the "drill and kill" model of teaching to the test. If students learn the basics of the following, we will be light-years ahead:

1 Learn to examine assumptions and premises;
2 Learn to examine alternate positions;
3 Learn to gather evidence and data to support positions;
4 Address conclusions from that evidence;
5 Be prepared to admit mistakes;
6 Learn how to connect knowledge with actual practice;
7 Learn to make connections between disciplines;
8 Learn how to synthesize information;
9 Learn how to offer critical analysis of subject matter; and
10 Learn to become a critical thinking and reevaluating person.

Moreover, in today's world, students have the opportunity to access all types of data bases and information on the Internet. In fact, a quick check of the Internet recently resulted in the following Web sites devoted to critical thinking, all of which offer advice and examples of good critical thinking

models to maintain high standards in the disciplines. Here are a few:

www.criticalthinking.org
www.utc.edu/teaching
www.wannalearn.com

In addition to the Internet, numerous books are valuable tools for enabling students and teachers to practice critical thinking approaches. For example, the use of portfolios of all types may be one of the best techniques to enhance critical thinking. The use of writing activities and critically reflective journals are other tools to enhance critical thought.

A Major Contradiction: The New Discrimination

What is most distressing about centralized, standardized testing is how it masks ongoing inequality. As McNeil (2000) and others point out, minority students who are already disadvantaged become invisible. As the curriculum narrowly focuses on test preparation, a new kind of discrimination emerges. Instead of outright tracking and stratification, the new discrimination uses the *appearance of sameness* to cover up inequalities. Most of the "basics" or "back to basics" mantra is historically rooted in the mistaken notion that sameness produces equity. Nothing could be further from the truth. Is there any evidence that standardization brings up the bottom scoring students? One would have to look very far and wide to find evidence for this given the evidence in McNeil's (2000) text. In fact, she argues persuasively that the TAAS system is actually harming students, teaching, curriculum development, and the faith and trust in public schooling. However, this situation reflects the unsurprising result of a system that places more faith in corporate business than in public schools. McNeil (2000) argues that substituting repetitive exercises for rich curriculum in poor and minority population schools is the *new discrimination*. Even if standardized "drill and kill" exercises raise scores in the present moment, children's learning is rarely enhanced or enriched. Worse, if Texas is any guide, any criticism of this new form of discrimination is dismissed as misinformed, confused, or unenlightened. The point Horn made as mentioned earlier in this chapter, about underreporting of dropouts, for example, teaches us about the dangers of denial. Denial perpetuates the problem rather solves the problem.

Some Hope for the Future

All educators struggle with issues regarding standards, testing, assessment, and evaluation. However, now there is a grassroots movement of parents, educators, and students concerned about these issues organized under the banner of FAIRTEST. Via their Web site, www.fairtest.org, this group has increased awareness of these issues by offering the history of the standards movement, reform movements, testing movements, and criticism of those movements. It also catalogues the activities of the states which are members of the ARN, the Assessment Reform Network. States are listed and evaluated as to the level of high-stakes testing being conducted and how citizens have organized to fight this mindless and rampant testing. Concerned citizens in California, Ohio, and Iowa, for instance, have fought high-stakes testing by removing students from the classroom on high-stakes testing days, by writing letters to local newspaper editors, and by holding meetings in public places to confront administrators about the ethics of standards and testing. On the Ohio Web site, a list of activities describes organizing a march on the legislature. In fact, fairtest.org lists sample letters to editors, descriptions and accounts of meetings, and how to get organized in your state. This Web site is living proof of many citizens coming together to build community by showing their deep concern for education. In doing so, critical thinking is not just critical thinking but also critical action.

With fairtest.org as the leader in monitoring what goes on nationally, it was not long before students also joined the discussion. In fact, students own and operate the Web site Students Against Testing at

www.nomoretests.com. Perhaps the most insightful summary I have seen to date about the NCLB legislation is on this site. (It's "speak truth to power" sincerity gave me the hope to write this book.) For example, the students have a section on the site listing 100 things to do INSTEAD of standardized testing. I cannot list all 100 activities, but to name a few, they describe writing an autobiography, designing a Web page, building some furniture, rebuilding a computer, taking a bike trip, interviewing the school janitor, helping someone, reading the newspaper, and making history. The students who work on this site also use humor to explain what has gone wrong with standardized tests. In fact, they spoof testing with their own "Best Standardized Test Ever." Here are a few examples from the spoof page:

1   The Texas Miracle proved
    a Country music makes kids smarter
    b All we need to do is kick out the low scoring
       and minority students
    c Testing is the same as learning
    d Y'all can't think for yourself
2   The scores of students most accurately reveal
    a Their parents' income
    b Their ability to explore the world
    c The number of nose hairs they have
    d How many doses of Prozac they were given the
       week before
3   True or False (and nothing in between)
    a In the end we need tests to hold schools
       accountable
    b The 4th grade MCAS is longer than the
       Massachusetts bar exam (true)
    c There is nothing I can do to change the testing
       craze in our schools
    d One day, you will discover the reason you
       had to take so many tests
    e Tests are graded carefully by well-trained staff
       at testing corporations

EXTRA CREDIT: (*hint: you just might get even more state money if you do this!*)

1 Create your own educational system.

2 List everything you would do right now if you didn't have to take this or any other test.

Obviously, these students are tapping into their humorous, creative side. However, they have also diligently scoured databases to list, for example, the organizations opposed to high-stakes testing much like the ARN has done. They have also summarized the research surrounding high-stakes testing and its problems to make it understandable to students and parents so that all may act on the information. In fact, they are completely accurate on the dangers of NCLB. Let us turn to the NCLB law as it is unavoidable given our discussion.

On the Folly of No Child Left Behind

It is really amazing that government employees and businessmen have the audacity to meddle in the work of professional educators and in that process demean and criticize the nearly entirely female work force. Would they do this in the field of medicine or law? Would they try to do this in engineering or the arts? The fact is the field of education is easy to pick on. The critics' reverie to the "good old days" is astonishing when one looks at the evidence. Were there ever any good old days? In addition, the media seem to love stories about failures in public schools. Is it not surprising that failures in private schools receive little if any press coverage? For example, a faith-based private charter type school in Florida was found to be ludicrously wanton in its use of public funds. The pompous promise of higher achievement was not met and, in fact, the students in this publicly funded private venture were actually described as below standard. However, rather than leading the national news, this case in Florida was only covered by local news media. CNN covered the story, but its report was brief and uninformative This minimal media coverage is not surprising given the planned attack on public education begun by the Reagan administration in the 1980s. NCLB has its his-

torical roots with Reagan policies and beliefs that continue today to attempt to:

1. Denigrate public education in order to move toward an agenda of privatization and corporatization of public schools;

2. Eradicate the U.S. Department of Education (thwarted, but no doubt will be tried again);

3. Develop an ongoing repertoire of public education failure stories while collecting little on private schools and their failures;

4. Use high-stakes testing as the only measure of effectiveness;

5. "Dumb down" tests to make it appear that more students pass the tests;

6. Marginalize people, programs, and research which offer solid evidence of the waste and mindlessness of high-stakes testing. For example, in April 2002, the Bush Administration conducted an Internet scrubbing of the ERIC data base of educational research, basically erasing all the research which did not agree with the administration's policy on education and testing. Furthermore, in remarkably poor taste, the Bush team went on to actually blacklist researchers and label them as unscientific despite the fact that their research was meticulously scientific by all such standards.

7. Remove teachers from actually teaching the subject matter of the curriculum in order to prep for high-stakes testing;

8. Threaten teachers with the corporate creed of "If you pass the test, you get the big money; if not we publicize your school as a failure";

9. Use high-stakes tests as a cover-up for what is really going on with dropouts, special needs students, minority students, and children whose native language is not English;

10. Foist on the public the erroneous belief that more tests make better schools;

11. Conceal the profits and conflicts of interest of companies making millions of dollars from the testing business, such as in Florida, where the

Florida test, FCAT, was owned and operated by Neil Bush, the brother of the Governor of Florida and the brother of President Bush;

12 Deny research which shows clearly all the problems with high-stakes testing and its effects;

13 Lead the public into thinking that one size fits all when it comes to testing;

14 Paint all regions of the United States—Northeast, Southeast, Deep South, Southwest, West, Northwest, North Central, and Midwest—as equal in terms of curricula;

15 Dishonestly report drop out rates to mask minority dropout rates;

16 Lower the bar for state testing requirements.

Sadly, even with the voices of Berliner and Biddle, Alfie Kohn, Susan Ohanian, the professionals at FAIRTEST, and all of us who write about the problems of high-stakes testing, the public is largely unaware of what the nature and harm of high-stakes testing is. In the meantime, hopeful signs continue to spring up. States that have experienced the serious and harmful effects of high-stakes testing are taking control of their education systems and saying "no more." In the resources section of this book, you will find many Web sites more fully described, but some sites from the states fighting the mindlessness of high-stakes testing deserve separate discussion.

At one site, The Florida Coalition for Assessment Reform (FCAR), www.fcar.org, you find a historical record for monitoring, exposing, and publicizing the problems with high-stakes testing and the NCLB law. Members of FCAR work to:

1 Monitor the uses and abuses of the FCAT;

2 Advocate for Florida's children;

3 Promote public policies that support constructive, authentic assessment;

4 Increase public awareness of alternatives to high-stakes testing; and

5 Publicize the onerous burdens and negative effects of NCLB.

These are reasons for hope. Similarly, Ohio has a site constructed by activist educators and parents at www.stophighstakestesting.org, also called www.stopopts.com, which is described as a central resource center to stop the Ohio Proficiency tests. At these sites, sample letters to send to congress, businessmen, and particular textbook companies (which have recently changed textbooks to match the state tests) can be found. These textbook makers do not allow for the use of creativity or imagination in the learning process. Sadly, they have trivialized learning by reducing schooling to memorizing facts, drilling for the facts, and trying to get that one right answer. Thus the books and tests are actually formulated to keep children from exercising critical and higher-order thinking skills.

To cite just one more example, let us turn to California. California educators and citizens organized the comprehensive site www.calcare.org where the Coalition for Authentic Reform in Education is battling against high-stakes testing and ethical improprieties in the administration and scoring of the standardized SAT-9 test while exposing testing's harmful effects and cultural biases.

When trying to make sense of the NCLB policy of high-stakes testing as a panacea for all of our school's problems, I turn to the great historian Barbara Tuchman (1912–1989). Tuchman wrote the text *The March of Folly from Troy to Vietnam* (1984) in which she argued that policies throughout history—from Troy to Vietnam—reveal leaders who blindly follow folly to disaster. According to Tuchman, a policy is folly if:

1   It is counter-productive at the time it is implemented;
2   There exists a feasible alternative course of action; and
3   The policy is a result of a single person or group rather than meaningful consultation.

As I review the literature and research on high-stakes testing, the love affair with standards, and the

marginalization of educators from educational activities, I see folly. Folly exists in the NCLB enterprise. It attempts to make all children fit one size. We already know that one size cannot, does not, and will not fit all.

In summary, there are a host of problems associated with NCLB. Many states are dealing with these problems by mobilizing parents, students, advocates, politicians, and local school personnel. What this demonstrates is that average citizens are concerned about the problems associated with NCLB and want school reform. They do not want the reform promised by NCLB and which is yet to be demonstrated. Rather, they want reform based on local input and following from the many research studies which may guide that reform.

GLOSSARY

Multiple-choice tests—multiple-choice tests usually have many test items. For each question, the test taker selects one answer from a given list of four or more choices. Most standardized tests are made up of multiple-choice items

Issues Related to Assessment

*. . . Under the look of fatigue. The attack of migraine and the sigh,
there is always another story, there is more than meets the eye.*
W. H. Auden
At Last the Secret is Out (1938)

When speaking of authentic assessment, there is
agreement on one of its outstanding characteristics: authentic assessment is ethical and fair. In
addtion, there is general agreement that high-stakes
testing is frequently unethical and is regularly unfair.
Authentic assessment is fair because it gives all students the opportunity to show what they can do.
Furthermore, authentic assessment is precise. The origin, purpose, importance, and meaning of assessment
is spelled out with clarity in many of the texts or
resources listed at the end of this primer. Thus,
ethics is a key issue related to authentic assessment.
At the same time, standardized testing provokes
many ethical problems. These are documented in the
literature and include the following:

1 Problems with the construction of the test;
2 Problems with the scoring and interpretation of the tests;
3 Problems with penalties for students who "fail" the test;
4 Problems with questions based upon cultural knowledge;
5 Problems with teaching and prepping for only the test; and
6 Problems with the high financial cost of testing.

Along with these ethical issues are other concerns, such as the use of power, how we classify people, the issue of diversity, and the greed by test making corporations. As the great philosopher Foucault (1979, 1994) has accurately pointed out:

> People write the history of experiments on those born blind or wolf-children or those under hypnosis. But who will write the more general, more fluid, but also more determinate history of the examination? Its rituals, its methods, its characteristics and their roles, its play of questions, and answers its systems of marketing and classification? For in this slender technique is to be found a whole domain of knowledge, a whole type of power.

As Foucault points out, divergent facets come together when we classify people, and this classification is mainly about power. Authentic assessment is a valuable tool for showing what *any* student can do. This approach flies in the face of some power structures, but imagine the possibilities if we were serious about what *all* students can accomplish. To say that we can now empower the student radically reshapes assessment, testing, evaluation, and accountability.

Wiggins (1998) argues that equitable, fair, and authentic means of assessment exist. He offers us a new way to assess our students. Here are some of his major guidelines:

1 Assess each student's accomplishments and progress, not merely the total score that results from points subtracted from a collection of items. In other words, score longitudinally

toward exemplary performance at various tasks, not by subtraction from "perfection" on simplistic and isolated tests.

2   Devise a scheme that assigns degree-of-difficulty points to assignments and test questions, thereby distinguishing the quality of performance from the degree of difficulty of the task.

3   Give all students the "same" demanding work, but scaffold assessments differently based on equitable expectations.

4   Devise a sliding grading system wherein the proportion of what is counted over time varies. Give weight to effort, progress, and achievement.

5   Have actual, live people—teachers—evaluate performance tasks rather than a machine scoring coded answer sheets.

Wiggins (1998) and others suggest that we can test students and still maintain standards, yet still be fair, ethical, and equitable in the process. There is no need to harm minorities, special education students, or ESL students. The growing body of evidence which demonstrates the unfair practices of high-stakes testing, for example, gives us cause for concern. For nearly thirty years, professionals in education and assessment such as Grant Wiggins (e.g., 1998), Monty Neil, Susan Ohanian (1999), Alfie Kohn (e.g., 2000) have shown where the harm lies and how to approach a remedy. That politicians and corporations refuse to look at the data is alarming and harms everyone. All of us lose when corporate profits and greed trump research, and educational philosophy and practice.

Some Related Facts on Assessment

Public schools in the United States have been scrutinized regularly and since the 1950s Cold War era persistent and vocal calls for reform continue to the present. The mass media and newspapers seem to enjoy focusing on negative reports on schooling. Consequently, activist educators have gone on the offensive to take up a reform agenda based on research and practices that work.

Activist Educational reformers are committed to:

1   Making schools better for students;
2   Using authentic assessment techniques to show what a student can do;
3   Avoiding nonethical testing procedures;
4   Responding to critics with solid results;
5   Imagining a way to use only appropriate testing to supplement the techniques of authentic assessment.

Although I have recounted some of the complexities of these issues earlier, there remains an important and critical consideration about assessment that relates to language. I am speaking of the need to be careful with language, not just because of the political consequences of these [r68]words (as shown in the Texas case), but also because of the emotional consequences of these words. Words such as "failing school," "a failing school for two years," and "accredited under review," are a few examples of language use which causes emotional reactions and political consequences, in Texas, to use just one example. (See Horn & Kincheloe, 2001) If we are to take seriously proposals about assessment of authentic tasks, we need to be aware of the social and political effects of language. Language is about power. How we use language is also about power. A skillful use of language that is not injurious is needed in the process of evaluating, assessing, setting standards, and measuring. This notion is also reinforced by the organization FAIRTEST, whose Web site is a resource on many aspects of authentic assessment. One important notion includes an agreement to do what is best for children by agreeing on standards to be used in assessing student achievement. FAIRTEST has addressed this subject on its Web site, where the National Forum on Assessment listed "Principles and Indicators for Student Assessment Systems" in order to help guide assessment reform. FAIRTEST used surveys to gather data, along with follow-up interviews and selected document review. FAIRTEST

adapted the "Principles and Indicators" to create appropriate standards for large-scale assessment. As listed on the Web site, they are:

Standard 1: Assessment supports important student learning;
Standard 2: Assessments are fair;
Standard 3: Professional development;
Standard 4: Public education, reporting, and parents' rights; and
Standard 5: System review and improvement.

Thus, FAIRTEST uses the principles of authentic assessment to reassess where schools are going. There is a continuous loop of trying something, reviewing it, and then improving it. They emphasize the need for fairness and diversity so that minority students, students whose first language is not English, and special education students are not listed as failures. Rather, these students should, in all fairness, be assessed with authentic measures to show what they too can do. All the research on this point indicates that one size does not fit all. It never has, and never will.

Authentic Assessment in Today's World

The politics of schooling most often gets in the way of student progress. Bureaucrats want a score in most cases. They want to measure the progress of students with one-shot prepackaged tests as if one size fits all. These tests cost money and take up sizable percentages of a school district's budget. Yet we know that many of these tests:

1   Do not match the curriculum of the school;
2   Do not test thinking or critical skills; and
3   Do not give a true picture of the entire scope of a student's abilities.

In schools, issues of fairness were applied to only the most basic activity of learning, how we assess what students know. It takes much more time, effort, involvement, teacher training, and teacher professional development to put authentic assessment

techniques into practice. Since the 1980s, educators have been clamoring to know more about authentic assessment in every state in the country. Why? Put simply, because it makes sense. Do we want our children judged and graded by one-shot tests which provide a simple score, or would we rather have our students assessed and graded by performance tasks that show not only what they learned but also what they can do? The reasons for preferring authentic assessment are solid and clear:

1   Authentic assessment overall is fair. No one racial or ethnic group is penalized with a one-shot score;
2   Authentic assessment tells a great deal about how students connect content knowledge to a given problem in the student's world;
3   Authentic assessment overall provides feedback on students' progress;
4   Authentic assessment shows how a student constructs a product or performance so that student growth can be seen;
5   Authentic assessment overall provides for continual feedback, allowing the student to adjust and improve performance;
6   Authentic assessment gives students a real, participatory stake in the learning process;
7   Authentic assessment de-emphasizes memorizing facts and repeating them; and
8   Authentic assessment allows performance tasks for evaluation.

These are not the only reasons to select authentic assessment as a solid evaluative technique. In today's world, students are bombarded with media images and information technology and, one might say, a virtual information explosion. The needs of today's student are more demanding, a bit more realistic, and a bit more challenging and competitive. This is all the more reason to give the student the opportunity to display what he or she has learned through performance-based authentic tasks. Many students today are sophisticated in the use of tech-

nology. Why not use this technology to assist the student in tracking the student's own progress in any given set of intellectual learning tasks? As mentioned in the first chapter of this primer, electronic portfolios, for example, offer a way to integrate and use technology for performance-based authentic assessment.

Ethical Issues Related to Assessment, Testing, and Evaluation

As to ethical issues related to high-stakes testing, the literature is filled with evidence which shows that:

1 There is one thing about standardized testing that is objective: The fact that all the scoring is done by machine;
2 Tests are filled with items that are biased, contain offensive words to some cultures, and are out of step with the curriculum;
3 Since standardized tests are predominately multiple-choice format, and each item has only one answer, many items are distractors. Thus, the element of subterfuge and trickery is regularly present;
4 Most test makers assume that those who take the test are white, middle-class students;
5 Standardized tests are taken as a one-shot activity. A student may not go back and edit or correct answers;
6 Standardized tests simply do not reflect how students learn today;
7 There are better ways to evaluate students; and
8 Because class time is consumed by test preparation, curriculum content is not taught as it should be.

But while all of these issues contribute to the ethical corruption of public education, the corporatization of public education injects yet another major ethical concern. Unbridled corporate test-making greed has further corrupted the morality and ethics of education.

The High Costs of Testing

The literature amply documents the exorbitant costs of high-stakes standardized testing (see, for example, www.fairtest.org.which lists related research on this topic) To cite just one recent example, consider the so-called "New" SAT "Writing" test. Some call it "painting new lipstick on an old pig": The new test is actually a repackaged old test. It contains outmoded and biased items. (More on the SAT below.) Worse, we already know that high-stakes testing costs up to $50 billion per year. The cost of developing, publishing, administrating, maintaining these test, not to mention tutoring, preparing, and scoring them has gone haywire. Think about the fact that the cost of high-stakes testing is equal to or higher than the gross national product of some countries. Baines and Stanley (2004) estimate that 14% of every dollar spent on the public schools goes into high-stakes testing costs.

One of the most costly of standardized tests is the high school exit exam. Take Minnesota for example. It costs an estimated $171 per student per year to implement the high school exit exam form. In Massachusetts, the cost is $385, and in Indiana the 10th grade test is $557 per student per year. It is important to realize, however, that the hidden costs of testing actually represent the bulk of the testing cost. These hidden costs include remedial and tutoring services for students labeled as "failures." Other costs go for teaching teachers how to teach to the test—what is euphemistically called "professional development." The euphemism for professional development is sometimes known as "test preparation." In addition, if we look closer, there is an added cost per student per year if the student is a student with a disability, or if the student is in the process of learning English. For example, the cost for this is as follows: In Minnesota, the cost is an additional $26. In Massachusetts it costs an extra $110. Evidently, test makers are making money on these tests. (The Center on Education Policy, www.cep-dc.org, has more information regarding these issues.)

It is clear some are obviously profiting from all this testing. It is not so clear to what extent students benefit from it.

Other Standardized Tests with Problems: The SAT

Perhaps the most controversy in assessment and testing is sparked by the costly Scholastic Aptitude Test, the SAT. Soon after a well-publicized decision by the University of California President, Richard Atkinson, to eliminate the SAT I for college bound students in February 2001, the following phone interview was printed verbatim in the *Chicago Tribune* on February 25, 2001. Although the SAT I had long been criticized for not being a reliable predictor of college success, the interview provides a unique exposé of the SAT "education-industry complex."

Q: Universities have been depending on scholastic aptitude tests forever to the point at which they have shaped American high school education. Why change that course now?

A: I think this is a debate that is long overdue and I think we have been making a mistake with the emphasis on the SAT I test. Hopefully, the debate that goes on among the faculty will be heard around the country.

Q: You are basically saying get rid of it?

A: Yes, I am. That doesn't mean I don't have a high regard for the Educational Testing Service [which develops and distributes the test]. They have the expertise and experience. On the other hand, the basic concept of the Scholastic Aptitude Test One is a mistake. It dates back to the 1930s, when most people thought we had a technology that allowed us to measure innate ability, and that was the goal of the initial test. The same strategy that led to the origins of the SAT I in the 1930s is still a part of that test today.

Q: But without the Scholastic Aptitude Test One as a gateway for college admissions, what standard should be applied?

A: Clearly we as a country have talked about a set of core subject matters taught at the high school level that we would expect the typical student to have mastery over, and those are the subject matters that should be tested. There will be coursework and grades from the classroom, too. In algebra, for example, to have a standardized test that the student took, the same test that everyone else took, would be a way of calibrating whether that classroom experience was really accomplished by the student.

Q: **But does that tell you about the student or about the test or, more specifically, about the school?**

A: It tells you about how much the student learned in that course. Obviously sitting down for a half-hour test is not enough to tell you about a student's accomplishments in high school. The high school grade based on coursework is one of the best things for that. We use these tests as a supplement to see whether there is anything that contradicts the grades.

Q: **What kind of test would you develop?**

A: It would be a series of tests that would focus on the curriculum that the student was exposed to in school. They would include algebra, writing skills, basic science skills. The student would clearly understand and the parents would clearly understand what the subject matter is that is being tested.

Q. **People have been upset about the pressure the SAT process created forever. Why hasn't change happened before now?**

A: In a sense, we have had the debate in sporadic ways, but without any effort to conclude it. And at times, people have wanted to link this to issues of affirmative action and the like. I think the debate has to be carried out independently of that discussion. The question is what is the best way to determine the opportunities that the student has in high school and what is the best way to try to use these tests to determine what

happens in terms of the teaching experience for the students in schools.

Q: Would eliminating the test transform attitudes in public education?

A: I would hope it would go some distance in helping us to focus on curriculum materials rather than to bypass those and prepare students just to take the SAT test. I am a product of the Chicago area. I went to Oak Park-River Forest High School and the University of Chicago. At the U. of C., SAT tests were not required when I entered. I entered the University of Chicago after two years of high school and it was one of those remarkable experiences. They don't do that anymore.

As many colleges begin reviewing their admissions testing requirements in response to University of California President Atkinson's call for the UC system to drop the SAT I, a new analysis by the National Center for Fair & Open Testing (FAIRTEST) has found that nearly 700 bachelor degree-granting institutions already admit substantial numbers of their applicants without regard to SAT I or ACT scores. Over 700 colleges do not use SAT I or ACT scores to admit substantial numbers of bachelor degree applicants. The FAIRTEST list includes such highly selective institutions as Bates, Bowdoin, Connecticut, Dickinson, Franklin & Marshall, Mount Holyoke, and Muhlenberg Colleges as well as large public systems in Iowa, Kansas, Texas, and other states. Religious, for-profit, and specialty colleges are also included. Of course, individual college and university Web sites list what is required of applicants. However, a full list of bachelor's degree-granting institutions that do not use the SAT I or ACT to make admissions decisions about substantial numbers of freshman applicants is posted by FAIRTEST at http://www.fairtest.org in both state-by-state and alphabetical order. In fact, FAIRTEST provides a wealth of information related to the ethical, legal, and political implications of standardized testing.

The Greed of the Test Makers

The SAT I test, also known as the Writing test, was known as a failure because it did not measure what it claimed to measure. Those particularly hard hit were minorities and those outside the mainstream. What did the test makers do? They recast the same sad test into the new SAT II Writing test! Now over 2.5 million students take the "new" writing test—with a new and improved fee of $41.50 (up from $12.00). In this way, the College Board (the organization responsible for SAT testing) reaps additional money to the tune of $30 million per year. It is allegedly a nonprofit organization, but data from U.S. Internal Revenue Service documents for the fiscal year ending June 30, 2003, reveal the College Board president, Gaston Caperton, a one-time insurance salesman and former Governor of West Virginia, received the nonprofit salary of $478,547, benefits of nearly $77,000, and an expense account of over $100, 000. However, if you think this is excessive, wait until you see the table below for the SAT manufacturing partner, the Educational Testing Service, ETS, based on a June 30, 2003, reporting.

ETS OFFICERS

Position	Name	Salary	Benefits	Bonus
President	Kurt Landgraf*	$405,000	$32,642	$350,000
Senior VP/CFO	Frank Gatti	$317,000	$23,438	$196,214
Senior VP	John Oswald	$356,711	$11,918	$30,170
Senior VP	Mari Pearlman	$231,000	$35,708	$99,000
Exec VP	Sharon Robinson	$326,983	$26,698	$15,900
VP/General Counsel	Stanford von Mayrhauser	$255,833	$27,255	$114,963
VP	Leslie Francis	$220,197	$27,192	$156,171
Chief Info. Officer	Arthur Chisholm	$252,083	$30,455	$266,000

* The ETS president also had an expense account allowance of $91,597.

The cost of standardized testing is exorbitant. However, the results are at best nonexistent and at worst harmful to some groups of students. Do we

really need to continue this dysfunctional approach to evaluation?

ETS and the College Board, though, are not the only groups that seem to profit from all that testing. Consider the McGraw Hill Companies, the primary contractor for Florida's state testing company. After Neal Bush's company was under fire for profiting from Florida's testing program, McGraw Hill (a leading U.S. test making company) landed a three year $82 million award from the Florida Department of Education to serve as the contractor for the FCAT from 2005–2008. This award includes a two year $58 million option to renew for 2008–2010. Furthermore, the Grow Network of McGraw Hill is the unit responsible for assessment and testing. Grow Network works with CTB McGraw Hill—the nation's leading publisher of standardized tests used by K-12 students. Grow Network is part of a global network of information services providers with more than 280 offices in more than 37 countries. Sales in 2004, for these tests, were $5.3 billion. To say that testing is costly is an understatement.

Summary

There are many problems associated with standardized testing. Encouraging large corporations to profit from standardized testing compounds these problems. Understanding some of the social, political, ethical, and legal dimensions of testing, we can more easily understand why authentic assessment is a solid alternative for educators, teachers, students, and parents. Standardized testing, whether K-12 or the SAT, exacts a high cost both financially and emotionally. The people who profit are the educational industry profiteers. Students, teachers, administrators, and parents are left with only the promise of so-called "high standards."

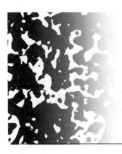

National Voices on Authentic Assessment

"In oneself lies the whole world and if you know how to look and learn, then the door is there and the key is on your hand. Nobody on earth can give you the key or the door to open, except yourself."

J. Krishnamurti
You are the World, 1972

Because authentic assessment as an alternative to high-stakes testing is a topic on the minds of educators, parents, students, and some technocrats, you can imagine that, state by state, district by district, people are making their voices heard. One of the ways people are being heard is in the courts. Lawsuits are being filed, discussed, and analyzed in regards to NCLB. These suits bear on a number of educational issues, one of which is authentic assessment as a viable alternative to high-stakes testing. The volume of law suits and areas of law revolving around NCLB are so extensive that I can only highlight a few states and their ongoing responses. We begin with Texas whose citizens, early on, started contesting critical legal

issues under the banner of educational malpractice. Because the Texas case is so well documented, I begin there, supplementing Texas with descriptions of other key states and their legal actions.

The Texas Fiasco

Of all states, it is ironic that Texas—President Bush's gubernatorial alma mater—provides the most evidence in terms of research and facts indicating that high-stakes testing is a dismal failure. The court cases consistently reveal who is least advantaged by NCLB. To summarize, the victims of high-stakes testing include:

1   Minority children, especially black and Hispanic students, who drop out of school but are not listed as dropouts;
2   Minority students living in poverty;
3   Minority students for whom English is not the first language of home or culture;
4   Special education students, whether minority or majority;
5   Any student who happens to transfer into a district with a curriculum that is unlike the curriculum of study in the previous state or district; and
6   Any student who lives in a state like Michigan, where the standard is higher than the federal standard for what counts as "passing" the test.

Since the 1990s, Texas parents, educators, and researchers (listed in the book bibliography below) have exposed the flaws in the previously-called-TAAS-now-renamed TAKS. Let us turn to the important cases which are a challenge to the NCLB, so well documented in the Horn and Kincheloe (2001) text.

Michigan

In Michigan, a pioneer in state-level accountability based on local and variable curricula, educators were shocked in 2002 to have so many failing schools. As it happens, Michigan had higher standards than the federal standards if only because federal standards themselves had been lowered so as to appear to be more user-friendly to minorities and special education students. In this way, Michigan schools were penalized for their higher standards by being labeled a "failure." It did not take long for Michigan to lower its passing grade for the high school English test from 75% to 42%, thereby reducing the number of failures from 1,500 to 216. For additional information see the State Of Michigan Department of Education web site. Other states learned how to play this game and followed the fine example of Michigan. For more information on this see the FAIRTEST Web site for state by state summaries, Teaching to the test is one problem; tampering with standards to fix the results is another. Standardized testing, however, sets both of these self-defeating processes in motion.

Pennsylvania

In Pennsylvania, educators decided to do the American thing and simply go to court. They decided it would be best to select a complaint which had a chance of winning in court. Part of NCLB legislation requires states to make progress on a test which is widely disputed due to issues such as unfairness, cost, and questions on federal jurisdiction. At the same time, however, the federal government does not fund the mandate. How does a school district go to court, then, to fight the claim that its schools are either not making adequate yearly progress ("AYP") or that they are failing? A school district in Pennsylvania, the Reading School District, decided to take its complaint not against the federal government but rather complain and sue the state of Pennsylvania. The reasoning behind this tactic, was to insure that the issue would be at least taken up in a state court.

The district argued that because 64% of the student population in the Reading School District is Hispanic, but the Pennsylvania State Department of Education provided no evaluation examinations in

Spanish, the conclusion that the Reading School District failed to achieve AYP cannot be evaluated, no less substantiated: Many of the students could hardly be said to have genuinely *taken* the exam, so how could they possibly fail it? To make matters worse, the penalty for AYP noncompliance is that federal funding is withdrawn. Given that the state is not making up the difference, and Reading has a weak tax basis, the school district is in serious financial trouble.

In the meantime, the National Education Association ("NEA") has approached the Reading School District to continue a court challenge against NCLB because the provisions of the federal law are unfair, unrealistic, and costly. The focus is on inadequate funding, a topic other states are taking up and marching to court with.

California

As is typical of California, the Golden State continues to try new approaches to attacking NCLB. In the *California Law Review, July 2004, 92 Calif. L. Rev. 117,* Melanie Natasha Henry, J. D. explains educational malpractice as the frontier of twenty-first-century litigation. The seminal case, *Peter W. v. San Francisco Unified School District,* illustrated how the courts were reluctant to require educators to conform to a duty of care. Consequently, a group known as Concerned California Citizens filed a suit against both the California State Board of Education and the school district. Arguing that NCLB specifically required "highly qualified" teachers, they found a loophole by which to bring suit. The plaintiffs argued that on May 30, 2002, the California State Board of Education knowingly and purposefully adopted a regulation that instituted a "lower" standard for the so-called "highly qualified" teachers, thereby violating NCLB. In response, the Board adopted a new proposal in June 10, 2003 that redefined "highly qualified" to meet the federal NCLB standard. What the California case teaches us is that educational malpractice suits are an effective tool that force state technocrats to take notice. Various states are pursuing educational

malpractice suits challenging the legality of NCLB and its implementation in the following ways:

1   as tort litigation;
2   as a violation of due process;
3   as a violation of constitutional rights;
4   as school finance inequality and equal protection;
5   as contract law violation;
6   as property law; and
7   as deprivation of civil rights

Now that the many flaws in NCLB have been documented, both individual citizens, including parents, and coalitions, are organizing to continue the legal challenges. For more specific information, the data links at the FAIRTEST site and the Assessment Reform Network Web site at www.arn.com can be consulted.

Florida

Florida has numerous lawsuits pending. One noticeable case has been brought by a parent whose child is a high-performing, high-achieving student. When the parents were informed that their child "failed" the FCAT, they made what they thought was a simple request: They asked the principal of the middle school for a copy of the FCAT. This simple request provoked a disproportionate amount of controversy and consternation, yet another symptom of a dysfunctional educational system. It turns out the principal refused on the assumption that it was illegal to disclose the test as it might be copied and distributed. Of course this perplexed the parent, since his child was a high achiever throughout the child's schooling, so he went to court to sue the State of Florida. This case has not yet been settled, but it does illustrate the veil of secrecy that shrouds so much of standardized testing. Authentic assessment is not like that. Authentic assessment encourages communication, sharing, and openness. The secrecy is totally unwarranted of course. Using authentic assessment, the student would know up front what the expectations for performance were. Much like the dancer or the ten-

nis player, the student would clearly know what is expected in training and in the final performance aspects of either dance or tennis. For the dancer in a dance company, the choreographer discloses early on the steps, the patterns, the emotional expectations of a given dance before rehearsals begin. Then in rehearsal feedback is given on these matters. Next the dancer implements the feedback and so on. In the end, the dancer is ready for the performance. In the case of tennis, the player learns to volley, to serve, to use various strategies, and to focus on the mental aspects of tennis, prior to playing in games and in competition. The coach of the tennis player gives continual feedback and reinforcement like the choreographer or the teacher. In these cases secrecy is out of place. As a result, everyone is a winner.

These cases offer a glimpse of grassroots action against NCLB and standardized testing. In order to track ongoing developments, FAIRTEST and the Assessment Reform Network Web sites list the activist coordinator assisting parents, teachers, students, and educators in getting information about assessment for each state.

Parents Getting Active in Assessment Reform

In addition to local state coordinators, parents are getting active as well and have created helpful documents for anyone to tailor to local requirements. The following is a sample FOIA letter requesting testing information created by a parent from Ohio (reproduced from the FAIRTEST Web site which includes other sample letters):

Date

Mr./Ms.
Title
Department
Agency
Address
City, State Zip

Mr./Ms. _____:

Freedom of Information Act (FOIA)

This act passed by Congress and signed by the President in 1966, gives members of the public the right to obtain certain government records. The law was written to contribute to an informed citizenry so that they could better participate in democratic decision making. States have their own FOIA laws and regulations which pertain to state and local government agencies. In order to use FOIA, a letter detailing the information sought must be sent to the appropriate record keeping department. If you are not sure where to begin, consult your state legislator's Secretary of State office for guidance.

I would like to request copies of the following information under the **Freedom of Information Act,** and as a request as an Ohio citizen. Could you and the Ohio Department of Education (EDO) please provide me with copies of any and all documents that discuss, evaluate, or state the appropriate and validated, or the inappropriate and invalidated, uses of the data resulting from all of the Ohio Proficiency Tests (fourth grade, sixth grade and ninth grade). Examples of this type of information would be discussions and evaluations of using the 4th grade test to determine grade promotion, or the appropriate use of the data to compare academic quality between school districts. I would also like to request copies of any documents stating or referring to test takers rights. It is likely that some of the types of documents which may include this information are (but not limited to):

1   The initial request for bid/proposal documents that were submitted to test writers/contractors stating what the tests are to measure. In other terms, the scope of work and objectives for developing the tests.
2   Contractual documents where the test contractor put in disclaimers or other statements related to the appropriate and validated (or inappropriate and invalidated) use of the test results, and test takers' rights.
3   Technical manuals written both externally and internally detailing the appropriate and valid (inappropriate and invalid) use of the test results, and test takers' rights.
4   Technical evaluation documents discussing and evaluating resultant data in terms of overall appropriate and validated uses of the data. These may be internal or external (outside contractor) documents.
5   Internal memos within the ODE or other state offices discussing these subjects or letters to legislators or other politically important people discussing these subjects.

Pursuant to [your own local FOIA law], we request a waiver of any and all fees for searching for and copying materials that respond to this request. Disclosure of the requested information is in the public interest, will greatly benefit the general public, and is not in the commercial interests of the undersigned or any other person.

It would be helpful if a time estimate could be given for submission of these documents to me. They are needed as soon as possible. Please feel free to contact me anytime with questions. A hard copy of this request will follow this facsimile in the mail. (Let the reader note that this is the letter which is used as a model since it was actually sent to relevant parties.)

California Strikes Again

Here is a sample of what California parents are doing as of the writing of this text. This is from their Web site at www.calCARE.org. California citizens have prepared a "helpful action" alert so teachers and parents can get involved in assessment reform. Some ideas include:

1 Circulate "know your rights" bulletins in your neighborhood;
2 Speak at a public meeting;
3 Be available to reporters;
4 Write articles for your newspapers;
5 Help pass out pamphlets;
6 Call other teachers and parents;
7 Host a meeting to get information to all;
8 Sponsor a CalCARE speaker;
9 Always be available to answer questions, so know the facts; and
10 Canvass your block and meet other parents.

This California site is very generous in offering assistance, phone numbers, and street and e-mail addresses. In addition, California parents have also created an "Opt Out of Tests" petition which encourages parents to publicly disavow standardized testing in the school. The petition states that the SAT

9/STAR tests administered in the California public schools are:

1 Racially, culturally, and socio-economically biased;
2 The pressure on teachers to teach to the test harms students as it narrows the curriculum considerably;
3 The state spends well over a billion dollars each year on the SAT9/STAR test while at the same time resources are cut on school supplies, personnel, and equipment;
4 The instructional time wasted is enormous;
5 We don't need the SAT9/STAR.

Massachusetts

Parental activism is also evident on the East Coast. In fact, it was a Massachusetts parent who began the organization known as CARE—the Coalition for Authentic Reform in Education. CARE is a statewide group of parents, educators, and citizens concerned about the impact of MCAS, the Massachusetts Comprehensive Assessment System test given to students in the state. CARE has conducted an analysis of MCAS test items, held a press conference to announce these findings, appeared on TV, written op-ed pieces for the papers and letters to the editor, co-hosted public forums, and met with legislators. CARE also hosts an e-mail discussion group with over 200 participants statewide, and their Web site, http://www.fairtest.org/arn/masspage.html, provides information about how to join e-mail discussions, CARE meetings, and CARE activities. Both a *Statement on the MCAS and Education Reform* and a collection of short "position papers" on related issues (such as accountability and alternative assessment) are also available.

One of the best points made on the Massachusetts site is how high-stakes testing affects our most vulnerable populations. In effect, we are blaming the victim when disadvantaged students are labeled as "failures." Activism is in the air—a sign of the grow-

ing dissatisfaction with high-stakes standardized testing and the corporatization of schools. From state to state, activists urge the following:

1   Look closely at your standardized tests;
2   Support rigor and excellence;
3   Resist misuse of tests and test results;
4   Work in partnerships to fight for assessment reform;
5   Support and learn from communities that are using effective assessment reform; and
6   Never lose hope.

Summary

In this chapter I have reviewed some of the key points regarding lawsuits brought against states for high-stakes testing improprieties, the activist nature of local reform efforts, and important state activities. It offers us hope for the future and a reminder to never give up the cause. State coordinators were listed as well as a sample of a Freedom of Information Act request letter to get information on the tests used in any state. Also, the California reformers offer step-by-step guidelines to working at the grassroots level on assessment reform. The point here is that there are existing models for the reader to access and possibly use in the future.

GLOSSARY

Freedom of Information Act (FOIA)—The Freedom of Information Act passed by Congress and signed by the President in 1966, gives members of the public the right to obtain certain government records. The law was written to contribute to an informed citizenry so that they could better participate in democratic decision making. States have their own FOIA laws and regulations which pertain to state and local government agencies. Depending on state FOIA laws, some or all of the following may be public documents subject to FOIA requests, others may be "exempt" form disclosure: a state's initial request for test creation proposals and selection criteria for contracting decisions, test validity and reliability studies, scoring procedures, cut-score or level setting procedures

(such as how failing scores are determined), expenditures, the type and cost of training provided for teachers to learn alternative assessment practices, the cost of benefits awarded to high scoring schools, the cost of holding students in a grade, a breakdown of test scores by race, class, gender, and socioeconomics. In some states, the contract with the test manufacturer may also be a public document. In order to use FOIA, a letter detailing the information sought must be sent to the appropriate record keeping department. If you are not sure where to begin, consult your state legislator's Secretary of State office for guidance.

Conclusions and Thoughts for the Future

Perhaps the greatest of all pedagogical fallacies is the notion that a person learns only the particular thing he is studying at the time.
John Dewey

If I had to select one major idea regarding the heart and soul of authentic assessment it would be this: Authentic assessment ensures that students are not bystanders but actual participants in the educational process. Authentic assessment requires students to think critically by using experience-based activities to solve a given problem. As a natural evolution, authentic assessment requires that the student be able to describe, explain, and justify the understandings surrounding any given problem. Thus, the student cannot and should not be asked to dumb down education by merely reciting or memorizing facts disconnected from a context or from an experience. If we seriously employ authentic assessment performance tasks, we would definitely give up the "drill and kill" exercises. For example, not long ago I visited a

third-grade urban classroom where students were shouting out loud the words "Don't bubble C! Bubble in B!" Because they were preparing for high-stakes standardized tests, the teacher was getting them to realize that most standardized tests often have the letter "B" answer as the correct choice. This is irrespective of the fact that all choices could be correct. What the student ends up learning is how to beat the system with little or no understanding of what the content of the question contained. And this is to be expected. Research on the Texas TAAS showed an alarming trend of trading content work to test preparation. However, what are children actually learning here?

Authentic assessment requires what John Dewey described as "habits of mind." Children who have solid habits of mind resonate with authentic assessment techniques. They learn

1   from experience;
2   in a given context;
3   in a given learning community;
4   with a responsibility for improving their own performance;
5   Demonstrating through a performance task what a student can do.
6   That this approach would lead to understanding a concept of acquiring knowledge and not merely memorizing an isolated fact, a test maker, who is not a professional educator, deems to be a correct answer.

Authentic assessment is a much more rigorous approach to teaching and learning. Rather than developing good habits of mind, high-stakes testing encourages bad habits of mind. Is it any wonder that professional educators have denounced high-stakes testing as a model of evaluation? Furthermore, authentic assessment is an orientation that relies on empirical evidence concerning what students can do. Let's pause to take a look at the word *empirical*. The word *empirical* means capable of being verified by observation, or derived from observation and exper-

iment rather than theory. So when students actually demonstrate in the real world what they can do with a performance task, there is a subsequent growth and movement toward knowing something in context. On the other hand, what high-stakes testing has achieved, outside of making test makers rich, is impoverishing children's learning experiences.

Wiggins (1993, 1998) and I (Janesick 2000) have argued that students are like an apprentice to a craftsperson or a protégé to a master artist. As such, the student should have access to continual feedback, access to multiple ways and models of knowing, and an opportunity to reshape or refashion the performance or performance task. Similarly, earlier in educational history, John Dewey argued relentlessly for clear, public, specific criteria and standards for learning. Authentic assessment is an approach which does that outright. There is no secrecy with authentic assessment. Let's take an example from the arts regarding performance. As a choreographer earlier in my life, all the dancers in my dance company knew the so-called testing points in a given piece from the first day of rehearsal. They knew when they had to execute a particular formation or individual movement during rehearsal. Each dancer received individual feedback, and the company as a whole received feedback and notes for the next rehearsal and obviously for the performance before an audience. Thus, we can learn from the apprentice model and the mentor-protégé model in terms of schooling. Performance-based tasks require doing, immersion in the activity—not watching, spectator behavior. As the great choreographer Twyla Tharp (2003) pointed out in her famous text, *The Creative Habit,* creativity is not a once-in-a-while sort of event. It should be an everyday occurrence with its own routines. Thus, it is helpful to view authentic assessment as a creative action, for it involves the entire being of the student much like any artistic activity requires the entire being of the artist.

Final Thoughts

Educators would be well served to use authentic assessment techniques in classrooms. We know from research, experience, and plain common sense, that high-stakes testing is harmful to our children and our future as a nation. Authentic assessment offers the best viable alternative to one-shot high-stakes tests. It has been well documented that high-stakes test do only two things well:

1 High-stakes standardized one-shot tests make money for test makers, and
2 High-stakes standardized one-shot tests tell us the size of students houses and their family income. Many studies document the fact that all you need to know is the poverty level of a school to determine with about 90% accuracy the results on such tests. (See Meier et al. 2004).

Likewise, we know that high-stakes testing gets quite a bit wrong:

1 High-stakes testing gets learning, growth, and development wrong;
2 High-stakes testing gets child development wrong;
3 High-stakes testing gets special education, bilingual education, English as a foreign language, and minority issues wrong;
4 High-stakes testing does not measure deep critical thinking or test multiple intelligences;
5 High-stakes testing does not show how students creatively connect the dots between main ideas and what they are learning; and
6 High-stakes testing does not respect creativity, imagination, or common sense.

Thus after reading this primer and taking into account the many resources, Web sites, research reports, lawsuits, and what we know about children, is it not time to look at the best alternative, authentic assessment?

References
and Resources

In this section, an extensive list of resources on authentic assessment is provided. Many organizations committed to authentic assessment are listed, though in a primer text not all organizations can be listed. The list represents a good start for those interested in authentic assessment. Similarly, key resources in print and nonprint forms and on the Internet are also provided. The volume of material listed even in this introductory guide is an indication that authentic assessment is one of the major foci within education today. Many descriptions for the websites have been summarized from or are verbatim descriptions from the Web Site.

Organizations That Provide Information on Assessment

American Association of Colleges for Teacher Education (AACTE)
1307 New York Avenue, NW, Suite 300
Washington, DC 20005–4701
202–293–2450, ext. 561
fax: 202–457–8095

e-mail: kmccabe@aacte.org

www.aacte.org/award.html

The American Association of Colleges for Teacher Education (AACTE) provides leadership for the continuing transformation of professional preparation programs to ensure competent and caring educators for all America's children and youths. It is the principal professional association for college and university leaders with responsibility for educational preparation. It is the major voice, nationally and internationally, for American colleges, schools, and departments of education, and is a focus of discussion and decision making on professional issues of institutional, state, national, and international significance.

American Federation of Teachers (AFT)

555 New Jersey Avenue, NW

Washington, DC 20001

202–879–4400

www.aft.org

The AFT represents 900,000 teachers, paraprofessionals, school-related personnel, public and municipal employees, higher education faculty and staff, nurses, and other health professionals. It advocates national standards for education, the professionalization of teaching, and disciplined and safe environments for learning.

Educators for Social Responsibility (ESR)

23 Garden Street

Cambridge, MA 02138

800–370–2515

617–492–1764

fax: 617–864–5164

www.benjerry.com

ESR, sponsored by the owners of Ben and Jerry's Ice cream, provides resources and services for educators and parents, including books, curricula, and workshops and training on violence prevention, conflict resolution, intergroup relations, and character education. Their Resolving Conflict Creatively Program is highly regarded.

FAIRTEST

342 Broadway

Cambridge, MA. 02139

617–864–4810

www.fairtest.org

The National Center for Fair & Open Testing (FAIRTEST) works to end the misuses and flaws of standardized testing and to ensure that evaluation of students, teachers, and schools is fair, open, valid, and educationally beneficial. It is the largest data bank available on fairness in testing, problems with high-stakes testing and

NCLB, as well as a comprehensive site for links to key assessment reform sites. FAIRTEST is a center of information on all aspects of testing. It catalogues the latest action steps taken in every state and reports on coalitions to fight unfair tests. It also contains various fact sheets on NCLB and offers many solutions for parents. FAIRTEST also publicizes position statements, tracks research on this topic, and offers a sounding board. The director, Monty Neil, is one of the top experts on fairness in testing and assessment issues.

Maryland Assessment Consortium
13471 Campus Drive
Ijamsville, MD 21754
301–874–6039
e-mail: mailto:mdac1381@erols.com
www.newhorizons.org

Maryland has been a leader in the assessment movement, and Director Jay McTighe is one of the best known assessment speakers. He has written several assessment "classics," has made videotapes, and has published assessments the consortium developed.

National Alliance of Black School Educators (NABSE)
2816 Georgia, NW
Washington, DC 20001
202–483–1549
fax: 202–483–8323
www.nabse.org

The Alliance consists of black educators and community leaders whose focus is the equitable education of black youths. NABSE advocates through legislative practice, public awareness, network building, and professional preparation of educators.

National Association of Secondary School Principals (NASSP)
1904 Association Drive
Reston, VA 22091–1537
703–860–0200
fax: 703–476–5432
www.naasp.org

Established in 1916, the NAASP has more than 41,000 members and is the nation's largest school leadership organization for middle and high school administrators. It provides a wide range of programs, publications, and consulting services on such topics as instructional improvement, student government, and urban education. It also promotes the interests of school administrators in Congress and sponsors student-oriented programs such as the National Association of Student Councils, the National Honor Society, and Partnerships International.

National Association of State Boards of Education (NASBE)
1012 Cameron Street

Alexandria, VA 22314
703–684–4000
fax: 703–836–2313
e-mail: boards@nasbe.org
www.nasbe.org

The NASBE is a nonprofit, private association that represents state and territorial boards of education. Its mission is to strengthen state boards of education by serving and representing them in their effort to ensure quality education. In 1994, the NASBE conducted a study group on violence and its impact on schools and learning. Countering policy trends that rely solely on the expulsion of students caught with weapons, the NASBE's resulting report, *Schools without Fear,* called for addressing the U.S. youth violence epidemic on multiple fronts by "using a creative balance of preventive as well as punitive strategies that target the individual, the home, the school, and the community."

National Board for Professional Teaching Standards
26555 Evergreen Road, Suite 400
Southfield, MI 48076
810–351–4444
fax: 810–351–4170
www.nbpts.org/nbpts/

The National Board for Professional Teaching Standards is an independent, nonprofit, nonpartisan organization governed by a 63-member board of directors. Most of the directors are classroom teachers. The others are school administrators, school board leaders, governors and state legislators, higher education officials, teacher union leaders, and business and community leaders. Their mission is to establish high and rigorous standards for what accomplished teachers should know and be able to do, to develop and operate a national, voluntary system to assess and certify teachers who meet these standards, and to advance related education reforms for the purpose of improving student learning in American schools.

National Center on Educational Outcomes
University of Minnesota
350 Elliot Hall
75 East River Road
Minneapolis, MN 55455
612–626–1530
fax: 612–624–0879
www.coled.umn.edu/NCEO

It is self-described as providing national leadership in the participation and continuance of students with disabilities and limited English proficiency in public schools by helping to identify outcomes, indicators, and assessments that help monitor the development of students with disabilities. The Center provides training, resource materials, consulting services, and technical assistance to organizations across the country. It offers a broad list of publications, technical reports, self-study guides, directory of assessment projects, and a national network regarding assessment issues.

National Council for Accreditation of Teacher Education (NCATE)
2010 Massachusetts Avenue, NW
Washington, DC 20036–1023
202–466–7496
fax: 202–296–6620
www.ncate.org

NCATE is the teaching profession's mechanism to help establish high-quality teacher preparation. Through the process of professional accreditation of schools, colleges, and departments of education, NCATE works to make a difference in the quality of teaching and teacher preparation. NCATE is a coalition of 33 specialty professional associations of teachers, teacher educators, content specialists, and local and state policy makers. All are committed to quality teaching, and together, the coalition represents over three million individuals. It is the performance-based accrediting body for teacher education programs in higher education. NCATE offers on-line publications, policy briefs, and research studies.

National Middle School Association (NMSA)
4151 Executive Parkway, Suite 300
Westerville, OH 43081
800–528–6672
www.nmsa.org

NMSA is a 20,000-member professional organization of teachers, administrators, parents, educational consultants, and community leaders expressly focused on the needs of the young adolescent. In addition to an annual national conference, state conferences, workshops, and several networks such as the National Forum for Middle Grades Reform, NMSA provides professional development, consultant services, and a wealth of resources from books and periodicals to Internet links and newsletters. The Association sets national standards for higher education teacher preparation programs and is the leading international voice for middle school education.

National Staff Development Council
PO Box 240
Oxford, OH 45056
513–523–6029
www.nsdc.org

The National Staff Development Council is the major profes-

sional organization to focus exclusively on the professional development of educators and the organizational development of educational institutions. The NSDC holds an annual conference early each December, publishes the quarterly *Journal of Staff Development,* the monthly *Results,* and the *School Improvement Team Innovator.* The NSDC maintains an active connection with educational research and theory but keeps its approach very practical and practitioner-oriented. The NSDC specialty is bridging the gap between research, theory, and practice. Members are balanced between school personnel, private consultants, laboratory staff, and university faculty. NSDC has 36 states and provincial affiliates which provide local support to staff developers.

Relearning by Design
65 South Main St.
Building B, Box 210
Pennington, NJ 08534
609–730–1199
fax: 609–730–1488
e-mail: info@relearning.org
www.relearning.org

Relearning by Design helps educators build schools around the student's needs as a student. They also provide consultations, in-service workshops, professional development seminars, and national conferences to improve the ways that educational goals and means are organized and assessed. They regularly provide a variety of printed materials, publications, videotapes, audiotapes, and software on student assessment and curriculum design. Relearning by Design is headed by Grant Wiggins. Wiggins has devoted his life to working on authentic assessment, and does countless workshops on the topic. His numerous books and articles on authentic assessment have provided the groundwork for schools across the nation to improve assessment techniques. He is often called the father of authentic assessment. He writes about standards, assessment techniques, evaluation and educational outcomes.

Students Against Testing
www.nomoretests.com

This Web site provides updates by students researching the perils of testing and provides updates on NCLB. It is a refreshing documentation of student activism from elementary grades through college years. It offers also some humorous entries to point out the problems with high-stakes tests. The students' point of view is a remarkable way to see the follies of testing.

Related Key Organizations

The following organizations are major professional groups. While not solely devoted to assessment, assessment is relevant to these organizations. The annual meeting programs from these groups show a large portion of the program devoted to exploring multiple and competing conceptions of assessment.

The American Association for Higher Education (AAHE)
One Dupont Circle, Suite 360
Washington, D.C. 20036
Phone: 202–293–6440
Fax: 202 -293–0073
www.aahe.org

The American Association for Higher Education is a national professional organization which sponsors an Assessment Forum that identifies the 9 Principles of Good Practice for Assessing Student Learning. The AAHE has selected four campus assessment Web sites as being particularly useful. They are listed below with AAHE's annotations.

American Educational Research Association
1230 Seventeenth Street, NW
Washington, DC 20036–3078
202–223–9485
www.aera.net

The American Educational Research Association is concerned with improving the educational process by encouraging scholarly inquiry related to education and by promoting the dissemination and practical application of research results. AERA is the most prominent international professional organization with the primary goal of advancing educational research and its practical application. Its more than 23,000 members are educators, administrators, counselors, evaluators, graduate students, behavioral scientists, and directors of research, testing or evaluation in federal, state, and local agencies. The broad range of disciplines represented by the membership includes education, psychology, statistics, sociology, history, economics, philosophy, anthropology, and political science. AERA was founded in 1916, is a key site for information on the problems with high-stakes testing, and has a statement against high-stakes testing.

American Evaluation Association
16 Sconticut Neck Rd.
Fairhaven, MA. 02719
1–888–232–2275
www.eval.org

The American Evaluation Organization is an international, professional organization devoted to the application of program evaluation, personnel evaluation, and technology. All forms of evaluation are of interest. The organization seeks to improve evaluation practices as well as assessment techniques and research methods. It conducts an annual meeting and various training sessions throughout the year on a regular basis.

Association for Supervision and Curriculum Development (ASCD)
1703 North Beauregard Street
Alexandria, VA 22311–1714
800–933-ASCD
703–578–9600
fax: 703–575–5400
www.ascd.org

The Association for Supervision and Curriculum Development is a unique international, nonprofit, nonpartisan association of professional educators whose jobs cross all grade levels and subject areas. In their diversity, members share a profound commitment to excellence in education. Founded in 1943, ASCD's mission is to forge relationships in terms of teaching and learning for the success of all students. ASCD sponsors workshops, conferences, and professional development sessions. In addition, books, journals, and videos on topics of interest to educators are available. ASCD also sponsors numerous networks that help members exchange ideas, share common interests, identify and solve problems, grow professionally, and establish collegial relationships.

The following networks may by of particular interest to readers of this book:

Authentic Assessment
Contact: Kathleen Busick
Pacific Region Educational Laboratory, Suite 1409m
1164 Bishop Street
Honolulu, Hawaii 96813.
808–532–1900
fax: 808–532–1922

Designing District Evaluation Instruments for Math and Science Process Skills
Contact: Shelley Lipowich
Math/Science Consultant
6321 North Canon del Pajaro
Tucson, Arizona 85715.
602–299–9583
fax: 602–886–2370

Thinking Assessment

Contact: Sally Duff
Maryland Center for Thinking Studies
Coppin State College
2500 West North Avenue
Baltimore, Maryland 21216
410–396–9362

International Reading Association
Public Information Office
800 Barksdale Road
PO Box 8139
Newark, DE 19714–8139
302–731–1600
fax: 302–731–1057
e-mail: pubinfo@reading.org
www.reading.org

> The International Reading Association is a dynamic and diverse organization that includes classroom teachers, reading specialists, consultants, administrators, supervisors, college teachers, researchers, psychologists, librarians, media specialists, students, and parents. The Association has more than 90,000 members in 99 countries and represents over 350,000 individuals and institutions through its affiliated councils worldwide. The International Reading Association seeks to promote high levels of literacy for all by improving the quality of reading instruction through studying the reading process and teaching techniques. It also serves as a clearinghouse for the dissemination of reading research through conferences, journals, and other publications and actively encourages the lifetime reading habit.

National Center for Research on Evaluation Standards, and Student
 Testing (CRESST)
UCLA Center for Research On Evaluation
CSE/CRESST
GSE & IS Bldg. MB 951522
Los Angeles, CA. 90095–1522
310–206–1532
www.crest.org
http://cresst96.cse.ucla.edu/index.htm

> Funded by the U.S. Department of Education, Office of Educational Research and Improvement, the National Center for Research on Evaluation, Standards, and Student Testing (CRESST) is a unique partnership of UCLA's Graduate School of Education & Information Studies and its Center for the Study of Evaluation. The CRESST mission focuses on the assessment of educational quality, addressing persistent problems in the design and use of assessment systems to serve multiple purposes. Other distinguished CRESST research partners include the University of Colorado, Stanford University,

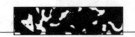

RAND, the University of Pittsburgh, University of California, Santa Barbara, and the Educational Testing Service. During its current funding period, CRESST research is organized into three programs of sustained R&D and one program for dissemination integrated into the research model on their website which includes: Teaching and Learning, Assessment, Policy and Outreach.

National Council of Teachers of English (NCTE)
1111 West Kenyon Road
Urbana, IL 61801–1096
800–369–6283
fax: 217–328–9645
e-mail: public_info@ncte.org
www.ncte.org

The National Council of Teachers of English, with 77,000 individual and institutional members worldwide, is dedicated to improving the teaching and learning of English and the language arts at all levels of education. Its membership is composed of elementary, middle, and high school teachers, supervisors of English programs, college and university faculty, teacher educators, local and state agency English specialists, and professionals in related fields. Members of the National Council of Teachers of English recently passed resolutions urging reconsideration of high-stakes testing and asking for the development of a test taker's bill of rights.

The resolutions were adopted by members attending the Council's Annual Business Meeting on Friday, November 17, 2000, in Milwaukee, Wisconsin. The new resolutions appear below. See the NCTE Web site (http://www.ncte.org/resolutions) for past resolutions.

Resolution on Urging Reconsideration of High-Stakes Testing

Background: The National Council of Teachers of English passed a resolution in 1999 expressing concern over the prevalence of high-stakes tests in the United States. The use of such tests has continued to escalate and to cause evident measurable damage to teaching and learning in US schools. Other professional organizations have likewise voiced strong objections to the use of a single test for making significant decisions. The NCTE is know for its leadership in voicing opposition to high-stakes testing which among other things states "that the National Council of Teachers of English affirm the following statement:

The efforts to improve the quality of education, especially in underachieving schools, are laudable, and the desire for accountability is understandable. However, high-stakes tests often fail to assess accurately students' knowledge, understanding, and capability. Raising test scores does not improve education. Therefore, the use of any single test in making important decisions—such as graduation, promotion, funding of schools, or employment and

compensations of administrators and teachers—is educationally unsound and unethical.

High-stakes testing often harms students' daily experience of learning, displaces more thoughtful and creative curriculum, diminishes the emotional well-being of educators and children, and unfairly damages the life-chances of members of vulnerable groups. We call on legislators and policymakers to repeal laws and policies that tie significant consequences to scores on single assessments. We further call on legislators and policymakers to join with professional organizations to develop better means of improving public education."

The NCTE has multiple and updated references, resources, resolutions and information regarding the harm of high stakes testing.

National Council for the Social Studies (NCSS)
NCSS Information Services
3501 Newark Street, NW
Washington, DC 20016
800–296–7840, ext. 106
e-mail: information@ncss.org
www.ncss.org/about/background.html

Founded in 1921, the National Council for the Social Studies has grown to be the largest association in the country devoted solely to social studies education. NCSS engages and supports educators in strengthening and advocating social studies. With members in all 50 states, the District of Columbia, and 69 foreign countries, NCSS serves as an umbrella organization for elementary, secondary, and college teachers of history, geography, economics, political science, sociology, psychology, anthropology, and law-related education. Organized into a network of more than 110 affiliated state, local, and regional councils and associated groups, the NCSS membership represents K-12 classroom teachers, college and university faculty members, curriculum designers and specialists, social studies supervisors, and leaders in the various disciplines that constitute the social studies. In the organization the group listed next goes even further in its opposition to high stakes testing. Here is an example of their statement, abbreviated here:

College and University Faculty Association of the National Council for the Social Studies Oppose High-Stakes Standardized Tests!

Whereas high-stakes standardized tests represent a powerful intrusion into America's classrooms, often taking up as much as 30% of teacher time,

And whereas the tests pretend that one standard fits all, when one standard does not fit all,

And whereas the high-stakes test pretend to neutrality but are deeply partisan in content.

And whereas the tests become commodities for opportunities whose interests are profits, not the best interests of children,

Be it therefore resolved that the National Council for the Social Studies join with the National Council of Teachers of English, the International Reading Association, and the American Educational Research Association in supporting long-term authentic assessment, opposing all high-stakes standardized examinations such as but not limited to the SAT 9 in California, the Michigan MEAP, the Texas TAAS, Florida's FCAT, and the New York Regents Exam. Moreover we support student and educator boycotts of the exams.

National Education Association (NEA)
1201 16th Street, NW
Washington, DC 20036
202–833–4000
www.nea.org

NEA members are trying to improve the situation of children and public schools. Sign up for the *NEA Focus,* the Association's weekly e-mail newsletter. Each week, subscribers receive late-breaking education highlights and news from national, state, and local levels. You'll also find links to valuable, related resources and concise information.

National Science Teachers Association (NSTA)
1840 Wilson Boulevard
Arlington, VA 22201–3000
703–243–7100
www.nsta.org

The National Science Teachers Association, founded in 1944 and headquartered in Arlington, Virginia, is the largest organization in the world committed to promoting excellence and innovation in science teaching and learning. NSTA's current membership of more than 53,000 includes science teachers, science supervisors, administrators, scientists, business and industry representatives, and others involved in science education. To address subjects of critical interest to science educators, the Association publishes five journals, a newspaper, many books, and many other publications. NSTA conducts national and regional conventions that attract more than 30,000 attendees annually. NSTA provides many programs and services for science educators, including awards, professional development workshops, and educational tours. NSTA offers professional certification for science teachers in eight teaching level and discipline area categories. In addition, NSTA has a Web site with links to state, national, and international science education organizations, an on-line catalog of publications, and two "discussion rooms" to foster interaction and ongoing conversations about science education.

Phi Delta Kappa International (PDK)
408 North Union
PO Box 789
Bloomington, IN 47402
800–766–1156
fax: 812–339–0018
www.pdkintl.org

> PDK is an international association of educators. The mission of PDK is to promote high quality education. Their emphasis is on publicly supported education as essential to a democracy. They sponsor professional development workshops regularly on all areas of interest to educators, including assessment. They offer a newsletter, a journal, *The Phi Delta Kappan,* a series of books, and travel seminars. PDK has been consistently tracking the problems with high-stakes testing and showing superb examples of authentic assessment and how to use authentic techniques.

Additional Web sites

Eastern New Mexico University Assessment Resource Office
http://W3a.enmu.edu/academics/excellence/assessment/index

> This site includes ten surveys used at Eastern New Mexico University, links to the New Mexico Higher Education Assessment Directors Association, and includes a section about the use of "CYBER CATS: Classroom Assessment Techniques" administered and reported via the Internet.

Educational Testing Services (ETS)
http://www.ets.org/aboutets/child/index.html

Education Commission of the States
http://nclb2.ecs.org/Projects_Centers/index.aspx?issueid=gen&IssueName=General

Education World: On-line Education News
http://www.educationworld.com/a_issues/issues273.shtml

ERIC Clearinghouse on Assessment and Evaluation
http://ericae.net/ftlib.htm

> The ERIC Clearinghouse on Assessment and Evaluation has opened the Text Internet Library. Here you will find links for full-text books, reports, journal articles, newsletter articles, and papers that address educational measurement, evaluation, and learning theory. It has documents based upon criteria that are widely accepted in the library and in the community and its framework allows for easy browsing.

Internet Resources for Higher Education Outcomes Assessment
http://www2.acs.ncsu.edu/UPA/assmt/resource/html

The Rural School and Community Trust
http://www.ruraledu.org/issues/nclb.htm

Student Outcomes Assessment at Montana State University
www.montana.edu.aircj/assess/techniques
> This Web site includes a list of suggested assessment techniques
> and assessment information for general education and capstone
> courses. Maintained by Cel Johnson.

Undergraduate Assessment & Program Review at Southern Illinois
University, Edwardsville
www.siue.edu/news/assessment
> This site offers extensive assessment information, including an essay
> entitled "Why do assessment?", an annotated bibliography of
> assessment resources, and thorough descriptions of primary trait
> analysis and classroom assessment techniques that can be used via
> the Internet. Maintained by Doug Eder.

University of Colorado at Boulder, Undergraduate Outcomes Assessment
www.colorado.edu/pba/outcomes
> This well-known site contains a comprehensive list of on-line
> resources. Browse down the page and click on "High Education
> Outcomes Assessments on the Web." This site was designed by
> Ephraim Schecter of Student Affairs Research Services.

Additional Web Sites on Specific Issues in Performance Assessment

Alternative Assessment for Adult Students:
> http://www2.nu.edu/nuri/llconf/conf1995/reif.html
> Article contains materials aimed at adult students.

Alternative Assessments: http://www.aurbach.com/alt_assess.html
> Materials provide definitions and characteristics of various alter-
> native assessment modes. Excellent listing of resources through
> hyperlinks.

An Introduction to Science Portfolios: http://www.gene.com/ae/21st/TL/
> This is mostly a biology Web site that explains the why and how
> of portfolios as well as guidelines from the California State
> Department of Education for portfolio use.

Assessment and Accountability: http://www.nwrel.org/eval/index.html
> This site is hosted by the NW Regional Lab (NWREL) and includes
> bibliographies of assessment information, a model writing assess-
> ment, and information about NWREL's "Alternative Assessment
> Toolkit" which is focused on the National Council of Teachers of
> Mathematics, NCTM, standards implementation.

Assessment related sites (index):
http://tiger.coe.missouri.edu/~arcwww/main.html

Assessment, Accountability, and Standards: http://www.serve.org/assessment/

Assessment: http://www.interactiveclassroom.com

Authentic Assessment Samples: http://www.miamisci.org/ph/default.html
The Miami Museum of Science-pH Factor includes other assessment
help and a "constructivist" approach to helping students learn.

Authentic Portfolio Assessment: http://www.teachersworkshop.com/
twshop/authen.html

Automating Authentic Assessment with Rubrics: http://stone.web.
brevard.k12.fl.us/html/comprubric.html

*Correlation between Degree of Standards-Based Implementation and Academic
Achievement:*http://www.srv.net/~msdata/nclb.html

Developing Educational Standards: http://putwest.boces.org/Standards.html

How to Assess Authentic Learning: http://www.business1.com/IRI_SKY/
Assess/htaali.htm

IMMEX Home Page (assessing problem-solving skills): http://night.
medsch.ucla.edu/

Index of National Assessment of Educational Progress: http://tiger.coe.
missouri.edu/~arcwww/main.html

Influence of Performance-Based and Authentic Assessment: http://www.
eduplace.com/rdg/res/literacy/assess2.html

Performance Assessment: http://www.cet.fsu.edu/

Sound Approach to School Improvement: http://nochildleft.com/h

NCLB-Related Web sites

Government Sponsored Web site
http://www.ed.gov/nclb/landing.jhtml
Government Legislation Web site
http://www.ed.gov/policy/elsec/leg/esea02/index.html
House of Representatives Education Committee Web site
http://edworkforce.house.gov/issues/107th/education/nclb/nclb.htm

Sites Providing Evidence of Flaws in the NCLB process

ARN Discussion Board
http://interversity.org/lists/arn-1 /archives/Apr2004/msg00077.html

Assessment Reform Network
www.arn.com

Association of Supervision and Curriculum Development Web site
http://www.ascd.org/portal/site/ascd/menuitem.f263fe58bc6e481edeb3ff
db62108a0c/#NCLB

Bridges for Kids Resource Site
http://www.bridges4kids.org/ESEA.html

Chicago Teachers Working for Social Justice
http://www.teachersforjustice.org/opposition.html

The Doyle Report (Tracks all the lawsuits against NCLB, especially PA,
CA, NY, MA)
www.thedoylereport.com

Florida Coalition for Assessment Reform
www.fcar.info
NCLBgrassroots.org
http://www.nclbgrassroots.org/
A Web site tracking news articles from every state on the No
Child Left Behind Act and monitoring how communities are far-
ing under the law.

Progressive Policy Institute
www.ppionline.org

Students Against Testing
www.nomoretests.com

Susan Ohanian Site
http://www.susanohanian.org/show_nclb_atrocities.html?id=1125

Videos on Performance-Based Authentic Assessment

ASCD 1996 Conference on Teaching & Learning: Assessment. Forums
with assessment leaders discussing the questions "What Have
We Learned about Performance Assessment?," "What Problems
Remain to be Solved?," and "What is the Relationship between
Assessment and Grades?" The site is www.ascd.org.

Assessment in Math & Science-What's the Point?, Annenberg/CPB Fall 2000
Video Catalogue. Individual programs:
1 Will this be on the Test? Knowing vs. Understanding
2 What'd I get? Scoring Tools
3 Is this Going to Count? Embedded Assessment*

4 I didn't know this was an English Class! Connections Across the Discipline
5 You WILL be tested on this: Standardized Testing
6 That Would Never Work Here! Seeing Assessment Reform in Action I*
7 That Would Never Work Here Either! Seeing Assessment Reform in Action*
8 When I was in School . . . Implementing Assessment Reform*
 * Pertains to assessment directly.

Assessment Interactive Training Multimedia Package, Phi Delta Kappa International Catalogue. This package created by Richard J. Stiggins of the Assessment Training Institute is designed to introduce educators to sound classroom assessment. Four, 60 minute videos cover all the bases on practical exercises for authentic performance assessment. The videos are:
1 Creating Sound Classroom Assessments
2 Assessing Reasoning in Classrooms
3 Student Involved Classrooms
4 Common Sense Paper and Pencil Assessments
All four videos are $799.00 available from Phi Delta Kappa International, P.O. Box 789, Bloomington, IN, 47402–0789, 1–800–766–1156, fax: 812–399–0018.

Performance Assessment in the Classroom by Jay McTighe, Director of the Maryland Assessment Consortium. Two videos for $295.00 produced by Video Journal of Education at 549 West 3560 S., Salt Lake City, UT 88441–4225. The Web site is http://www.videojournal.com

Performance-Based Assessment in Quality Elementary & Middle Schools by the National Association of Elementary School Principals (NAESP). Available for $189.95 for members at 1615 Duke Street, Alexandria, VA 22314–3483, 800–386–2377.

Redesigning Assessment, a "classic" three-part series including an introduction video, a more in-depth treatment of performance assessment and its impact on classrooms and learning, and a video on portfolios. Contact ASCD at 800–933-ASCD or www.ascd.org.

Standards, Not Standardization, a four-volume set of eight videos and training materials by Grant Wiggins's organization, the Center for Learning, Assessment & School Structure (CLASS). This is a non-profit educational organization in Geneseo, NY.

What's New in Schools: A Parent's Guide to Performance Assessment, includes examples of tasks, projects, and portfolios with comments by students, teachers, and parents. Includes a readers' guide. Contact ASCD at 800–933-ASCD or www.ascd.org.

A LIST OF STATE COORDINATORS FOR TESTING REFORM

State	Contact	E-mail	Phone
Alaska	Ken Jones	afkwj@uaa.alaska.edu	not available
Arizona	Gabie Gedlaman	ggedlaman@bigfoot.com	480–539–1337
California (northern)	Lysa Tabachnick	lysat@cruzio.com	831–469–4280
California (southern)	Rich Gibson	rgibson@pipeline.com	619–583–6886
Colorado	John McCluskey	McFort3@cs.com	970–484–5914
Connecticut	Pedro Mendia-Landa	pedro.mendia@yale.edu	203–439–8121
Delaware	Denise Davis	denisedavis@eclipsetel.com	410–755–6891
Florida	Gloria Pipkin	gpipkin@i-1.net	not available
Georgia	Lisa Amspaugh	amspaugh@excelonline.com	770–963–2431
Hawaii	Verlie Malina-Wright	vmalinawri@aol.com	808–261–3714
Idaho	Dan Kmitta	kmitta@uidaho.edu	208–885–7637
Illinois	Harvey Daniels	smokeylit@aol.com	312–441–6635
Iowa	Dick Hanzelka	dhanzelka@aea9.k12.ia.us	319–344–6301
Louisiana	C. C. Campbell-Rock	parentjustice@hotmail.com	504–948–6250
Maine	Bo Hewey	khewey@maine.rr.com	207–774–0419
Maryland	Bess Altwerger	altwerg@saber.towson.edu	410–830–3188
Massachusetts	Karen Hartke	khartke@fairtest.org	617–864–4810
Michigan	Rich Gibson	rgibson@pipeline.com	313–577–0918
Minnesota	Wade Nelson	wnelson@vax2.winona.msus.edu	507–285–7589
Mississippi	Libbie Love	llove@watervalley.net	662–473–9268
Missouri	Debra Smith	d_smith@vax1.rockhurst.edu	816–501–4148
Nevada	Chuck MacLeod	castausa@hotmail.com	775–826–7848
New Hampshire	Arthur Pelletier	ajpell@email.com	not available
New Jersey	Dee Bucciarelli	deenb@worldnet.att.net	609–924–3416
New York	Jan Hammond	jdh77777@aol.com	914–257–2812
North Carolina	Irv Besecker	besecker@sprynet.com	336–766–6160
Ohio	Mary O'Brien	sobrien@columbus.rr.com	614–487–0477
Oklahoma	Will Muir	wmuir@norman.k12.0k.us	405–364–4465
Oregon	Bill Bigelow	bbpdx@aol.com	503–916–5140
Pennsylvania	Melissa Butler	mab@icubed.com	412–421–1724
South Carolina	Andrew HaLevi	AHTeacher@aol.com	843–723–3734
South Dakota	Kim Hanes	khanes@sd.value.net	605–734–4052
Tennessee	Gilda Lyon	gdlyon@yahoo.com	423–825–0844
Texas	Eileen Weinstein	lilefty@aol.com	713–629–8233
Utah	Michelle Bachman	michelle.bachman@slc.k12.ut.us	801–485–5608
Vermont	Susan Ohanian	SOhan70241@aol.com	802–425–4201
Virginia	Mickey VanDerwerker	wmzemka@aol.com	540–586–6149
Washington	Juanita Doyon	Jedoyon@aol.com	253–846–0823
Washington, DC	Aleta Margolis	aleta@artistryinteaching.org	202–822–8081
Wisconsin	Bob Peterson	REPMilw@aol.com	414–265–6217

Note: This list is subject to change. If a state is not listed, it most likely is in need of a coordinator. If you would like to volunteer to act as coordinator of your state, please contact www.fairtest.org

References

A Nation at Risk: *The Imperative for Educational Reform,* 1983, http://www.ed.gov/pubs/NatAtRisk/index.html

Auden, W. H. (1976) Collected Poems. New York: Random House.

Baines, L. A. and Stanley, G. K. (2004). High-Stakes Testing Hustle: Public Schools and The New Billion Dollar Accountability. *The Educational Forum,* 68, 8–15.

Berliner, D. C. and Biddle, B. (1995). *The Manufactured Crisis: Myths, Fraud and the Attack on America's Public Schools.* Reading, MA: Addison-Wesley.

Cuban, L.(1990) Reforming Again and Again and Again. *Educational Researcher,* 19, n0.1:313.

DeGregory, L. The FCAT and the Hospital, *St. Petersburg(FL) Times Newspaper,* February 10, 2005.

Dewey, J. (1897). My Pedagogic Creed. *The School Journal,* 54 (3), 77–80.

Dewey, J. (1899). *The School and Society.* Chicago: University of Chicago Press.

Dewey, J. (1902). *The Child and the Curriculum.* Chicago: University of Chicago Press.

Dewey, J. (1910). *How We Think.* New York: D. C. Heath.

Dewey, J. (1916/1966). *Democracy and Education.* New York: The Free Press.

Dewey, J. (1934). *Art as Experience.* New York: Minton Balch.

Dewey, J. (1938). *Experience and Education.* New York: Macmillan.

Foucault, M. (1970). *The Order of Things: An Archeology of the Human Sciences.* London: Tavistock.

Fusarelli, L. D. (2004). The potential impact of No Child Left Behind Act on Equity and Diversity in American Education. *Educational Policy,* 18 (1), 71–94.

Gardner, H. (1993). *Multiple Intelligences: The Theory and Practice.* New York: Basic Books.

Gardner, H. (1999). *The Disciplined Mind. What All Students Should Understand.* New York: Simon and Schuster.

Goldberg, M. (2005). Test Mess 2: Are We Doing Better a Year Later? *Phi Delta Kappan,* 86 (5), 389–395.

Goodman, P. (1962) Compulsory Miseducation. New York: Random House.

Holt, J. (1964) How Children Fail. New York: Dell.

Horn, R. (2004). *Standards Primer.* New York: Peter Lang.

Horn, R. and Kincheloe, J. L. (2001). *American Standards: Quality Education in a Complex World, the Texas Case.* New York: Peter Lang.

Illich, I. (1971) Deschooling Society. New York: Harper and Row.

Janesick, V. J. (2001). *The Assessment Debate: A Reference Handbook.* Santa Barbara, CA: ABC-CLIO Publishers.

Kohn, A. (1993/1999). *Punished by Rewards: The Trouble with Gold*

Stars, Incentive Plans, A's, Praise, and Bribes. Boston: Houghton Mifflin.

Kohn, A. (1999). *The Schools Our Children Deserve: Moving beyond Traditional Classrooms and "Tougher Standards."* Boston: Houghton Mifflin.

Kohn, A. (2000). *The Case against Standardized Testing: Raising the Scores, Ruining the Schools.* Portsmouth, NH: Heinemann.

Kohn, A. (2004). *What Does It Mean to Be Well Educated? And More Essays on Standards, Grading, and Other Follies.* Boston: Beacon Press.

Lund, J. (1997) Authentic Assessment: Its Development and Application. Journal of Physical Education, Recreation, and Dance, 68,no 7, (September) 25–28.

Mallon, T. (1995). *A Book of One's Own: People and Their Diaries.* Saint Paul, MN: Hungry Mind Press.

McNeil, L. (2000). *Contradictions of School Reform: Educational Costs of Standardized Testing.* New York: Routledge.

Meier, D. (2000). *Will Standards Save Public Education?* Boston: Beacon Press.

Meier, D. A.Kohn, L.D.Hammond, T. Sizer, & G. Wood. (2004) Many Children Left Behind: How the NCLB Act is Damaging Our Children and Schools. Boston: Beacon Press.

Minkin, M. (2004). Test Ban Entreaty: An Interview with Alfie Kohn. *Hope Magazine* Jan.-Feb., 1–3.

Moore, R. & D. Moore. (1981) Home Grown Kids: A Practical Handbook for Teaching Your Children at Home. Waco, Texas: Word Books.

Ohanian, S. (1999). *One Size Fits Few: The Folly of Educational Standards.* Portsmouth, NH: Heinemann.

Orlich, D.C., R.J. Harder, R.C. Callahan and P.M. Taubman. (1995) *Teaching Strategies* Boston: Houghton Mifflin.

Orlich, D. C. (2000)   A Critical Analysis of the grade fourWashington Assessment of Student Learning. *Curriculum in Context.* 27,(2),10-14.

Paul, R. (1993). *Critical Thinking: How to PrepareStudents for a RapidlyChanging World.* Santa Rosa, CA: Foundation for Critical Thinking.

Progoff, I. (1992). *At a Journal Workshop: Writing to Aaccess the Power of the Unconscious and to Evoke Creative Ability.* Los Angeles: J. P. Tarcher.

Resnick, L.B. (1990) Literacy In School and Out. *Daedalus.*119 (2) pp.164–185.

Silberman, C. (1970) Crisis in the Classroom: The Remaking of American Education. New York: Random House.

Silver, H.F.,R. Strong, & M. J. Perrini (2000) *So Each May Learn.* Alexandria, VA: Association for Supervision and Curriculum Development.

Tharp, T. with Reiter, M. (2003). *The Creative Habit: Learn Iit and Use It for Life.* New York: Simon and Schuster.

Tuchman, B. W. (1984). *The March of Folly from Troy to Vietnam.* New

York: Bantam Books.

Weil, D. and Anderson, H. K., eds. (2000). *Perspectives in Critical Thinking: Essays by Teachers in Theory and Practice.* New York: Peter Lang.

Wiggins, G. (1993a). *Assessing Student Performance: Exploring the Purpose and Limits of Ttesting.* San Francisco: Jossey-Bass Publishers.

Wiggins, G. (1993b). Assessment: Authenticity, Context, and Validity. *Phi Delta Kappan,* 75 (3), 200–214.

Wiggins, G. (1998). *Educative Assessment: Designing Assessments to Inform and Improve Student Performance.* San Francisco: Jossey-Bass.

Peter Lang
PRIMERS
in Education

Peter Lang Primers are designed to provide a brief and concise introduction or supplement to specific topics in education. Although sophisticated in content, these primers are written in an accessible style, making them perfect for undergraduate and graduate classroom use. Each volume includes a glossary of key terms and a References and Resources section.

Other published and forthcoming volumes cover such topics as:

- Standards
- Popular Culture
- Critical Pedagogy
- Literacy
- Higher Education
- John Dewey
- Feminist Theory and Education
- Studying Urban Youth Culture
- Multiculturalism through Postformalism
- Creative Problem Solving
- Teaching the Holocaust
- Piaget and Education
- Deleuze and Education
- Foucault and Education

Look for more Peter Lang Primers to be published soon. To order other volumes, please contact our Customer Service Department:

      800-770-LANG (within the US)
      212-647-7706 (outside the US)
      212-647-7707 (fax)

To find out more about this and other Peter Lang book series, or to browse a full list of education titles, please visit our website:

      www.peterlang.com